PENGUIN BOOKS

ACTIVE LEARNING

As a Ph.D. engineer, Peter D. Lenn was teaching advanced calculus at the University of California at Berkeley when he became frustrated by his inability to be more effective as a teacher. Delving into educational psychology, he found powerful ideas that were just beginning to be used by the most forward-thinking companies in the United States. He soon founded his own training consulting company. Over the next twenty years he trained over 150 associates to learn quickly and to design effective courses for a variety of corporations and government agencies.

To assist his own children in school, he began adapting these approaches into a student success course for teenagers. These Active Learning courses for teens are now held like summer camps on college campuses each summer. Since 1986, as president and cofounder of Active Learning, Inc., Lenn has trained hundreds of teachers and thousands of parents to guide teens to success in school.

Lenn has written textbooks on such subjects as study skills, computers, and criminal law for peace officers. His teen program is featured in a Time/Life video course also called Active Learning.

For more information about Active Learning courses and videotapes, please call (800) 734-8336.

D1372181

·*Active*·
Learning

A Parent's Guide
to Helping
Your Teen
Make the Grade
in School

Peter D. Lenn, Ph.D.

Founder and President
Active Learning, Inc.

■ *Penguin Books* ■

PENGUIN BOOKS
Published by the Penguin Group
Penguin Books USA Inc., 375 Hudson Street,
New York, New York 10014, U.S.A.
Penguin Books Ltd, 27 Wrights Lane,
London W8 5TZ, England
Penguin Books Australia Ltd, Ringwood,
Victoria, Australia
Penguin Books Canada Ltd, 10 Alcorn Avenue,
Toronto, Ontario, Canada M4V 3B2
Penguin Books (N.Z.) Ltd, 182–190 Wairau Road,
Auckland 10, New Zealand

Penguin Books Ltd, Registered Offices:
Harmondsworth, Middlesex, England

3   5   7   9   10   8   6   4

LIBRARY OF CONGRESS CATALOGING IN PUBLICATION DATA
Lenn, Peter D.
Active learning: a parent's guide to helping your teen make the
grade in school/ Peter D. Lenn.
p.   cm.
Includes bibliographical references
ISBN 0 14 01.7653 5
1. Education—United States—Parent participation.   2. Parent and
teenager—United States.   I. Title.
LB1048.5.L46   1993
649.68—dc20   92–34814

Printed in the United States of America
Set in ITC Garamond

*Dedicated with love
to my wife, Natalie,
who has nurtured me,
our children, and
Active Learning*

Editorial Note

This book is addressed to all parents of teenagers. This includes single parents, stepparents, and parents who don't live with their teens, as well as to grandparents and guardians responsible for parenting teens.

For balance, we have referred to teens as "he" in Chapters 1, 3, 5, 7, 9, and the appendix, and as "she" in the introduction and Chapters 2, 4, 6, and 8. Similarly, we have attempted to balance references to mothers, fathers, and teachers of both sexes.

The anecdotes are about real teens and their families. The first and last names of parents, teens, and teachers have been changed to disguise the individuals involved.

Acknowledgments

Most of the ideas of and approaches to Active Learning are not mine. I have learned them from the research, writings, and teaching of others. Their work has produced today's state of the art in education and family dynamics. What I have done, with the generous and dedicated assistance of my colleagues at Active Learning, is combine and present those ideas in ways that have been understandable and practical for the families participating in our workshops and programs.

Since this is a practical book for parents rather than a textbook, I have provided only a few references to acknowledge the sources of key ideas and to let you know that solid research lies behind the Active Learning approach. But even with more complete footnotes and references, I would still have wanted to mention the authors who have been most significant to my work. In the field of family dynamics I have learned much from the works of Rudolf Dreikurs, Don Dinkmeyer, Haim Ginott, and

Thomas Gordon. In the realm of education and learning I owe a great debt to the ideas and work of William A. Deterline, James L. Evans, Robert F. Mager, Benjamin S. Bloom, and George Leonard.

The original development of Active Learning was a joint effort with Landon Carter, who, in addition to his energy and intelligence, brought his special ability to communicate to groups of all ages and his zeal for contributing to others. For several years, Lisa Kenney led and trained others to lead our parent seminars. Her contribution to the development of our approaches, as well as to bringing our ideas to thousands of families, was prodigious.

All of what I present here evolved over a period of years. Throughout that time, I had the opportunity to learn by doing, working with families who took a chance on Active Learning and me. I thank them for their contribution to my learning.

Of all the families I have been involved with, none has taught me more, nor had to put up with so many of my theories, than my own family. My wife, Natalie, has lovingly and consistently dealt with the immediate issues we faced with our children and helped me generalize our experience to others. Our daughter, Joanna, and our son, Josh, had no choice about participating in our training as parents. But they generously and wonderfully accepted their lot, and have been a constant source of pleasure and excitement to Natalie and me.

In the preparation of this book, I was greatly assisted by the comments and suggestions of my friends Judith

Greber, Wendy Drucker, Joel Renbaum, M.D., and Seymour Boorstein, M.D.; my brother, Nicholas Lenn, M.D.; and my agent, Patti Breitman. My editor at Viking Penguin, Lori Lipsky, provided key suggestions for using anecdotes about families in our seminars to make this presentation more readable and understandable. She also was kind enough and energetic enough to set what must be world records in publishing to make this book available at the same time as our Active Learning home-study videos for teenagers.

Contents

Introduction

Is This Happening at Your House?

This book is about what parents can do to help their teens succeed in school. It addresses situations like these:

- With great conviction Pete had said, "Trust me. I'll do better next semester." But he isn't.
- Mark's test scores indicate he should be at the top of the class. But he's bored by school and his grades are terrible.
- Jill gets A's and B's from teachers she likes, but C's and D's from teachers she doesn't.
- Byron is a couch potato. He seems listless and lazy about everything—school, social life, and hobbies. He watches a lot of TV and seems to have given up on himself.
- For Trina, who is vivacious and popular, school is interfering with her social life. Not only won't

her C-minus grades get her into a four-year college, but she might not have the skills needed to succeed in junior college.

- Sean is usually surprised by lower grades than he expected. He makes excuses and blames everyone but himself for his low grades and the minor troubles he gets into at school and at home.

- Having an older brother and sister, Beth is fourteen going on twenty. Maybe, because they both did so well in school, she is trying to stand out in her own way. She's really a neat, well adjusted kid, who does well in everything but school. So unless she starts hitting the books, she will not meet her own goal of following her sister to UCLA.

- Carlos is absentminded and disorganized. When he does his homework, he may not turn it in. Often he loses his notes about assignments or forgets to look at them. Even when he does study for tests, he seems to study the wrong material.

- Marla struggles with math and English courses. When her mom and dad try to help, it ends in an argument. She refuses to ask her teachers for help or to get a tutor. Even after an absence, she is reluctant to ask teachers what she has missed. As a result, she is getting a couple of D's, and may flunk math.

- Keith thinks he isn't smart enough to do well in school and mostly refuses to talk about it. He doesn't study at home. If asked, he either says there isn't any homework or that he did it in school. In fact, he just isn't doing it.

■ Christi is really diligent about her schoolwork, but she doesn't test well. Her grades are lower than she would like and don't reflect all the work she is doing. If she were more relaxed and self-confident, she would do much better.

If one or more of these teenagers seems like yours, this book is for you. It is not just about getting better grades in school—though grades tend to indicate when things are going well. This book is about helping your teen prepare for adulthood. It will show you how to guide your teen in learning to be well organized, self-confident, and responsible—able to handle school or any other project throughout her life.

Why Focus on School?

This book focuses on schooling rather than social life, athletics, or hobbies. Other areas of a teen's life are important, but school is a teen's full-time job. How a teen is doing in school affects her day-to-day happiness, as well as her overall self-image and self-esteem. In addition, because of parents' justifiable concern, school issues are a major source of friction in many families.

If you can help your teen succeed in school, there will be a halo effect in every other aspect of life. Each successful experience builds self-confidence and motivates further effort, which of course produces more success. Success breeds success. If your teen is having difficulties, especially in school, this book will show you how to avoid a vicious cycle of frustration, discouragement, self-doubt, and defensiveness or defiance. This book will show you how to get your teen started on the path toward success.

Where Did This Book Come From?

Before describing how you can help your teen, you might want to know something about me and how I developed the suggestions I have for you.

I grew up with the usual notions about intelligence —namely, that some people had it and some didn't. Within that framework, I was very intelligent, an outstanding student. I won math contests in high school and was accepted to M.I.T. with a full four-year scholarship. Even at M.I.T. I was an *A* student, and I won fellowships that paid my way through graduate school, to a Ph.D. as an engineer.

While working in the aerospace industry, I taught math and computer courses at night to engineers working toward a master's degree. I taught those courses in the way I had been taught, and my students did about as well as students usually do. In other words, some did very well, some did poorly, and most were in the middle. That result frustrated me, so I began to explore the literature on learning and educational psychology. What I found was both surprising and fascinating. Applying the latest research findings, I was soon a much more effective teacher. Shortly thereafter, I began writing training manuals and designing training courses for others, and then I started a company to develop training programs for adults in business: for bankers, policemen, college instructors, surveyors, salesmen, and others. In 1973 we won our first million-dollar contract to develop courses for the Army. That was just after the Vietnam War, when the draft was ended and many soldiers in the all-volunteer Army were high-school dropouts with fifth- or sixth-grade reading levels. Those volunteer soldiers with weak learning skills and poor academic records were our students. Our contract with the Army called for us to create self-study lessons to teach technical skills such as repairing radars and surveying. When we completed a set of lessons, the Army gathered thirty untrained soldiers and had them study without any help. When the soldiers were done, they were asked to perform the jobs they had just studied. If at least twenty-four of the thirty soldiers could perform successfully, the Army accepted our lessons and paid us. If not, we had to revise the lessons and submit them again for the same acceptance test.

At that time I still had my original notions about intelligence, and from that perspective, these soldiers were below average. So I worried that seven or more soldiers in each group of thirty simply wouldn't have the intelligence to learn the tasks, let alone from our self-study lessons. We might never get those lessons accepted. But over a period of eight years, in testing over five hundred lessons on over ten thousand soldiers, I completely changed my view. Intelligence was almost never a problem. These soldiers, high-school dropouts with minimal reading skills, were smart enough to master complex technical tasks. That's how I learned that almost everyone is smart enough to succeed in school. In fact, research shows that at least 95 percent of high-school students can completely master everything in the high-school curriculum.

I gained another important insight from training our own staff to learn the material our clients wanted us to teach. Almost all of us adults, regardless of how well we do in some fields, have other areas in which we feel we just can't learn or excel. For some of us math was like that; for others—like me—it was foreign languages or dancing. In our company, the writers were mostly teachers, journalism majors, English majors, and so on. So you can imagine that most of them felt pretty uneasy when they got an assignment to learn and write lessons in math or electronics or mechanics. But we devised a training program to teach them how to learn effectively—how to be Active Learners. That training program gave our company an enormous competitive edge. But it also made our writers feel terrific about themselves. They overcame doubts about their own abilities.

Here's one story to illustrate this point. Pat Cady was an experienced writer and editor in the field of English literature. Not suspecting she would have to learn and write about technical subjects, she applied for and got a writing job with us. After her training and a few other projects, we assigned Pat to develop a series of lessons on helicopter maintenance. Despite her training with us, the old gremlins haunted her. She was afraid she might not be able to learn this job, let alone write lessons that would teach others to do it. But she persevered, and she did fantastic work. In the final test, the students trained with her lessons passed with flying colors. Pat told me she had previously been intimidated by machines and was bothered by her own prejudice that men were better able to handle machines. She was thrilled to find that she could succeed in the mechanical realm, too.

When our daughter entered middle school, I started showing her the learning skills we were teaching our writers. Thinking that those skills might enable her and other teens to get more out of school with less effort, I adapted our company training program for high-school and college students, and tried it with fifteen students. The results convinced me that we had something of value, and so I continued to present and improve the Active Learning program. Since then we have had the privilege of working with over nine thousand families, with outstanding results. Over 80 percent of parents and teens who try Active Learning report significant improvements in school performance. More than 80 percent also report that the teens are more responsible, happier, and that parents and teens are getting along better with each other.

Active Learning at Your House

As we developed and refined the Active Learning program, we found that a most important aspect of our program was the information and methods we presented to parents in our parent seminars. This book is an attempt to provide that same information to you in a convenient and economical form.

You can assist your teen in developing the study skills and self-management skills of an Active Learner. You do not have to choose between being a permissive parent whose teen is an underachiever or being a disciplinarian who controls all aspects of an honor student's life. There is a sensible middle ground, based on love, empathy, communication, reasonable expectations, and high hopes.

This book will show you how to teach your teen to reach any goal one step at a time. As your teen practices and learns to be responsible for herself, you can relax and enjoy her and yourself. You can feel joy and pride in her learning, just as you did when she took her first steps. You can have pleasant days and a wonderful relationship as your teen makes the transition from dependent child to independent, responsible young adult.

Active
Learning

Chapter 1

The Barriers to Success in School

Getting in the Swim

Most people think it is natural and inevitable that only about 25 percent of students succeed in school. A hundred years ago, people thought that about swimming; they thought only a small fraction of people had the ability to swim. In those days, swimming was taught by tossing the student into deep water. Despite being highly motivated and actually making it back to shore, most beginners concluded that swimming was not for them.

Today swimming instruction is a gradual, step-by-step process with an almost 100 percent success rate. School isn't like that. Most teens are not succeeding in school. They feel they are in over their heads and are frustrated, angry, and perhaps discouraged. They aren't learning enough and they are getting mediocre grades. Even worse, poor high-school performance undermines their motivation, attitudes, and self-esteem and closes off important options for the future. And to top it off, parents, teens, and teachers are struggling and unhappy about the situation.

Typical Problems

Here are some of the typical problems teens have about school:

- They hate school.
- They often say they did the homework in school, or didn't have any today, when that isn't true.
- Sometimes they do the homework and then lose it or just don't turn it in.
- They won't talk about school, or the discussion often ends in a fight.
- They won't ask for or accept help from teachers, parents, a tutor, or anyone else.
- They do well in some subjects but not in others.
- They do well if they like a teacher, poorly if they don't.
- They are often surprised by low grades, do poorly on tests, and study the wrong material for tests.
- They make excuses, blame the teacher.
- They procrastinate a lot.
- They are disorganized and don't know the as-signments and due dates.
- They are unmotivated and often discouraged.
- They start out each semester with good intentions,

but don't follow through. They are easily frustrated and give up.
■ They are rebellious, cut school, get in trouble.

If you and your teen have struggled with one or more of these problems, this book can help you help your teen succeed in school. In the process you will both learn to work together to solve other issues: chores, curfew, driving, drinking, dating, sex, and money.

Just Get a Good Education

As parents we feel responsible for protecting and nurturing our teens as they grow into responsible, independent adults. We know they will have to learn from their own experiences, both successful and not. But we don't want them to have to learn everything in the school of hard knocks. To make their path easier, we try to give them the benefit of our experience and a good education.

So let's start by defining what we mean by a good education and success in school. Not necessarily in the order of priority, a good education includes:

■ Basic skills: reading, writing, and arithmetic.
■ Enough knowledge to cope with school and life. This includes some knowledge of such subjects as history, science, geography, government, literature, and business.
■ Reasoning and problem-solving ability.

- Learning skills for school and beyond, such as note-taking, test taking, studying from a text, memorizing, outlining, essay writing.
- Self-management: the ability to plan and organize, manage time, overcome procrastination, persevere, ask for help, correct mistakes, and deal with people and "the system."
- Good grades and test scores, both to build self-esteem and confidence and to open doors to college and career.
- Positive values and attitudes.

In addition to all of this, we want our teens to enjoy their youth. And we want to enjoy that time, too. We want to minimize the upsets and eliminate the feeling that we have to continually pull them, kicking and screaming, through school.

So success in school means more than learning the courses and getting good grades. It also means feeling successful and having the skills, discipline, and attitudes to learn new things throughout life. *An educated person is someone who knows how to learn.*

What's a Parent to Do?

When their teens are not getting a good education and being successful in school, parents often ask for advice for situations like the following:

- *I'd like to help, but my teen won't let me.* This is probably the most common situation. It is natural for parents to want to help and advise, and for adolescents to want to be independent. So teens resist interference by parents in various direct or indirect ways. Typical teens may say, "Trust me, I can handle it." Others range from being rude or argumentative, to being sullen and noncommunicative. A grandfather I know said of his two now grown-up children, "High school was four years of slamming doors and loud music. You can't talk to a teenager."

- *What can I do if I don't know the subject?* In one way or another, many parents feel unqualified to help their teens. Sometimes the subject matter is simply beyond what we know or remember. Or we may be understandably intimidated by the social and emotional stresses our teens face. There has been so much new research into education and child psychology, it seems that relying on one's own experience and intuition is probably less than optimal.

- *My teen probably blames the teachers too often, but how can I tell when the problem really is the teacher?* Lots of us have heard our teens irresponsibly say, "It's not my fault. Mr. Frank is a lousy teacher. None of the kids is learning anything. No one is getting better than a C in his class. All of us hate him." On the one hand, there are some poorly performing teachers. Maybe Mr.

Frank is one of them. On the other hand, you know your teen isn't exactly a model of diligence and organization. You suspect that some kids are learning in Mr. Frank's class. And you wish your teen would stop blaming Mr. Frank, whether fairly or unfairly, do the homework, and learn the subject.

■ *My teen said, "If I don't do better by midterms, you can ground me for the rest of the semester." He didn't, so he's grounded, but he still isn't doing any better. What now?* After vehemently declaring their good intentions, after promising to buckle down and do better in school, many teens have difficulty following through. They procrastinate rather than persevere. They sometimes stoically accept the consequences they proposed for not succeeding, to the point that a parent will say, "It hurts me to see him sitting home every weekend. It might not be so bad if it was helping, but it isn't. It seems too harsh to impose more restrictions, and ignoring the agreement we had seems wrong, too."

There are things you can do to solve or eliminate these problems. You can learn how with the guidance in this book and a little practice. But before trying to make things better, you need a workable understanding of the nature of the problem. Understanding the problems that plague many teenagers in school will allow you to be more effective as a parent. So before describing and recommending specific techniques and actions for parents, let's consider why most students aren't succeeding in school.

Some of the usual explanations are:

- Inadequate schools and teachers
- Low motivation; students having bad attitudes about school
- A lack of intelligence and/or talent in some subject areas

We'll examine these possibilities, but as you'll see, these are not usually the correct explanations. So after dispelling them, we'll focus on the real barriers to your teen's success in school—barriers you can help him overcome.

Fix the School

Even with all the attention on education, the schools are not going to get a lot better in time for your teenager. And even in the best schools, a large percentage of students are not succeeding. So fixing your teen's present school or transferring him to another one is unlikely to help. Your best bet is to help your teen succeed in school just as it exists today.

Motivation

Many of you recognize that your teens are not adequately motivated to do well in school. Some teens put off schoolwork for activities they like better, some do less than they should to excel, and some seem to refuse to work at all. So motivation is an important issue, which I will be addressing throughout this book. At this point, I just want to rule out two of the key elements of motivation that are not a problem for teens.

Motivation means that a person chooses to expend time and energy working toward some goal or purpose. If a person is not motivated in a particular area, some possible reasons are:

- He doesn't know what the rewards and benefits are.
- He knows the rewards and benefits but doesn't value them, or he does not value them highly enough to make the effort to earn the reward.
- He is lazy, due to some inherent personality or character flaw.

Many parents try to motivate their teens by addressing the first two issues. For example, many parents repeatedly lecture or remind their teens about the benefits of education. When their teens argue or ignore that advice, it seems to prove that teens don't realize the importance of education.

But the truth is that teens do know the benefits of education. The message from parents, teachers, and society in general has gotten through to all of them. They know that education provides opportunities for more income, status, and satisfaction. They realize that an educated person is better prepared to cope with life. The teen's seeming resistance to advice about school is more of a defense than a disagreement. And that is why teens often seem so unreasonable about school.

So no matter how your teen has been doing in school, and no matter what he says about school, your teen knows the value of education. You may think your teen is different, but believe me, your teen's performance in school is not hindered by his lack of appreciation for the benefits. Therefore, improving his motivation will not require explaining or convincing him of those benefits.

In our Active Learning programs, we have dealt with over nine thousand students. It has been our experience that no matter what the teens said when they entered the program, and regardless of their previous school records, essentially every one of those nine thousand students came to us already knowing that education is valuable. Once they overcame the various barriers they had erected to protect themselves in their struggles with school, they would not only listen, but could themselves do a good job of describing the benefits and of expressing their own interest in working toward getting an education. Please be assured that our program contains no inspirational lectures or compelling charts of life-time earning that "convinced" the teens of the value of learning.

In addition to our experience at Active Learning, there are numerous research studies in which students' efforts and results in school were greatly improved by things that had nothing to do with teaching the students more about the benefits and rewards of education. You have probably heard of some of those studies. Some studies involved falsifying student records so their teachers incorrectly believed their class to be unusually gifted or unusually slow. In other studies, student performance improved by teaching students study skills, or by promising money for college to low-income children. If the real barrier to success had been that teens don't value education, those results could not have been attained.

So, based on my experience, I suggest you make the following two assumptions about your teen and all other teens.

First, no matter what they say or how they are doing, all teens know the value of education. So you can let up on selling the benefits of education.

Second, your teen is not inherently lazy. He is willing to work to succeed in school. All teens would love to do well in school. Even those who seem uninterested or unconcerned often think about school performance. *School is a teenager's full-time job.* The school day plus an ordinary amount of homework, or just procrastinating about homework, add up to forty hours per week, forty weeks of the year. School success or failure, progress or boredom, while not the only important things in a teen's life, are very significant.

All teens have the basic human characteristics that

make people enjoy doing what they do well and avoid things they think they can't do. That's why success breeds success. Motivation comes from successes, rather than the other way around. As you'll see, Active Learning provides ways to help your teen get started, experiencing success in areas that were difficult in the past and in new areas.

We have considered and dismissed fixing the schools and trying to raise motivation through lectures or advice about the benefits of education. We have also dismissed the notion that your teen is lazy and unwilling to work for success in school. The final incorrect notion to be gotten out of the way is that school performance depends on intelligence.

Intelligence

Almost all teens believe school performance depends primarily on intelligence—on being smart or bright or a "brain." In addition, regardless of any high test scores or reassurances from you, most teens think they are not very intelligent. They tend to form harsh judgments of themselves as lacking in intelligence and motivation, as lazy procrastinators. When parents or teachers tell them they could do better if they would just apply themselves, they don't believe it.

As I said earlier, research has shown at least 95 percent of students have the intelligence to master everything in the high-school curriculum. In a variety of experiments, Professor Benjamin S. Bloom of the University of Chicago and others have demonstrated that almost everyone can completely master English, algebra, biology, and all the rest at the high-school level. That means they can not only pass the courses, but can actually master the material. They are smart enough to get A's. And those who master high-school coursework are almost certainly intelligent enough to do well in college.

It is true that there are differences in learning and thinking abilities between people. To some extent, those differences affect how quickly and easily we learn various subjects and skills. Those differences may also limit the ultimate level of ability we can attain. But school performance depends mainly on doing enough of the right kind of *practice*, rather than on intelligence.

This is an important point and one that may run contrary to your previous notions and contrary to your teen's view of himself. We know it is impossible to design an intelligence test that measures only intelligence. A student's performance on the test depends on factors other than his age, such as maturity and prior learning and practice. In *The Mismeasurement of Man*, Stephen Jay Gould, a professor of anthropology at Harvard University, documents the problems and mistakes that are made in measuring and evaluating people based on intelligence.

Just think of people you know whose exceptional abilities seem surprising in view of their school records. You might, for example, know someone in an unskilled job who has memorized an incredible data bank of sports information. Or you may know someone who has been unusually successful in business or some hobby but flunked out of college. Finally, notice that almost everyone in Spain is smart enough to learn Spanish. Learning Spanish, even as a second language, is primarily a matter of sufficient practice, not of intelligence.

So unless there is some specific evidence to the contrary, *you can safely assume your teenager is intelligent enough to do well in school and that most likely he doesn't think he is*. If you think your child may have a learning disability or a deficit in reading, writing, or arithmetic, there are some hints in the appendix of this book on getting a professional evaluation.

The Three Barriers to Success in School

So teens have more than adequate intelligence to master all their courses, they value education, and they want to be successful. Then why are the majority of teens underachieving? The answer is usually one or more of three barriers.

Resistance

In addition to the natural and normal need to become independent, many teens rebel against parents, teachers, and school. Being inexperienced but anxious to prove their maturity, teens are frequently unskillful and unsuccessful in getting what they want. For example, in attempting to gain control over their own curfew, they violate their present curfew. This causes parents to restrict them more—exactly the opposite of the result the teens were trying to achieve. In frustration and anger, some teens blame their parents for being overcontrolling and untrusting. The parents often respond with more controls, punishments, and anger. A pattern for counterproductive resistance is started that may persist for years and sometimes escalates to extremes.

Of course teens want independence and peer approval. But perhaps surprisingly and most significantly, teens also want and need to feel loved and admired by their parents. Because education is so significant for both parents and teens, teens may feel their parents judge them and value them on the basis of school performance. And since few teens feel very successful as students, most of them feel they are not meeting their parents' expectations. Some react with resentment, others with rebellion—two forms of resistance.

Parents often contribute to the problem by unintentionally giving too much advice and criticism, and too little approval and encouragement. As a result, many teens react in negative ways. So teens may act hostile, rebellious, shy, stubborn, lazy, forgetful, and uncooperative. Naturally, these negative behaviors rarely work and, when viewed objectively, could not be expected to produce the results the teens want. Still, teens do them in an effort to either get attention or to fend off unwanted attention. These actions constitute a barrier of resistance, which is frequently called teenage rebellion or a bad attitude.

Learning Skills and Background Knowledge

Many students lack basic learning and study skills. They don't know how to learn. They haven't the study skills and self-management skills—the equivalent of job skills—to succeed in school. These include time management, organization, memorization techniques, note-taking, and study methods. For the most part, these study skills are taught in school, though usually as parts of other courses. The students who master these skills are usually the same students who are mastering their other coursework.

In addition, many students move from grade to grade and from course to course without having mastered such basic skills as reading, grammar, composition, fractions, or decimals. These are prerequisites for subsequent courses, and the lack of these skills puts those students at an unfair disadvantage. The schools tend to ignore this issue, giving all students the impression that intelligence and hard work is all they need to get good grades. But a child who forgot or didn't learn fractions is not ready to succeed in algebra.

Self-confidence

Many students lack confidence as learners. Many teens don't think they have the intelligence and personality to compete with the really good students. Consequently, many won't try. Some are aware of their own low opinion of themselves as students, but they may not admit it to anyone. Other teens hold the same view unconsciously and so have only the vague feeling that school is the wrong place for them to shine.

For anyone in any endeavor, it is difficult to work hard without an expectation of success. And schools and teachers tend to put out the message that only a small percentage of students can succeed. Though the intention is to use competition and fear of failure to motivate students, the actual result is that many children and teens are discouraged rather than encouraged. Though many educators recognize this, a large percentage of them see no practical alternatives. So in the interests of motivating some and controlling many, they accept that some students will be discouraged. Unfortunately, in today's schools that discouragement is not just an occasional side effect but is the general experience of most students.

The children naively believe that any worthy student succeeds in school. So if they aren't succeeding, they come to the erroneous conclusion that there is something wrong with them, and they get discouraged or rebellious. Those reactions are often labeled a lack of motivation.

So the three barriers to success in school are active or passive resistance, lack of specific knowledge and learning skills, and a lack of self-confidence as a learner. By helping your teen become aware of these barriers and to get over, through, or around them, you will empower him to reach his full potential. You won't have to force or bribe him to do something he doesn't want to do.

Rather, your job is to help him overcome those barriers to making the most of himself. In the chapters that follow, you'll learn how to do that.

Here's a case history, typical of so many others, that demonstrates the effectiveness of focusing on removing the three barriers to success. Cliff was a good kid. He didn't get into any trouble and he was reasonably cooperative at home. The only problems he and his parents had were related to school. Cliff seemed to have no motivation to learn, did homework grudgingly and incompletely, and got grades much lower than his teachers and parents thought him capable of. It seemed to Cliff that his parents nagged him constantly about his homework. He felt angry and resentful about that and often thought to himself that he would do it if they would just let him alone.

His parents were concerned. It seemed that unless they kept after Cliff, he wouldn't do anything at all, that he would drop from C's to D's and F's. They had alternated repeatedly between reasoning, rewards, threats, and punishments. It seemed that nothing helped; Cliff only seemed to get more resistant. He sometimes lied, saying there was no homework; he procrastinated endlessly; and, most frustrating of all, he sometimes lost or forgot to turn in work he had actually completed.

Throughout ninth grade, the situation got worse. Cliff sulked, argued, and avoided conversation. He was trying to achieve independence by acting independent. Of course, to his parents, Cliff seemed irresponsible and diffident, rather than responsible and independent. So they kept trying to control and guide him. And the more they did that, the more Cliff resented and resisted being controlled.

As is typical in this type of counterproductive pattern, both Cliff and his parents felt they were just responding to the situation the other was creating. Both sides felt they would change just as soon as the other side allowed them to.

After using the Active Learning approach, Cliff's parents said:

It used to be a constant battle. "Did you do your homework? Did you do your homework?" Now he is very different, just in the way he talks to us. He used to sit not saying anything. Closed up. He probably always knew that he had to take responsibility for learning, that no one could do it for him. But now he verbalizes that. Now we never have to ask him if he's done his homework. Not ever. He just goes and does it. And the changes in his self-image are at least as pronounced as the changes in his grades.

And Cliff said:

I was always arguing with my parents. Now we can communicate because we know how to talk and listen to each other. That has changed everything in my family. My parents just don't bug or nag me and they say I'm easier to deal with. I've gone from a 2.3 to a 3.5 GPA. I feel more confident. I'm on the right track and that feels good.

Chapter 1 Key Points

1. A good education includes mastering the courses, learning how to learn, and building self-esteem, self-confidence, and responsibility.
2. At least 95 percent of teens have the intelligence to master all their courses. Most of them don't think they do.
3. All teens know the value of education and would love to be successful in school, which is their full-time job.
4. Just like everyone else, teens enjoy the things they do well and avoid those they think they can't succeed at. Successes build motivation.
5. The three barriers to success are:
   - Active or passive resistance to parents, teachers, and school; rebellious or resisting behaviors as a reaction to feeling incapable, unworthy, and therefore unlovable;
   - Lack of background knowledge and learning skills, including reading, writing, math, memorizing, studying, note-taking, time management, organizing, and goal setting; and
   - Lack of self-confidence as a student.

Chapter 2

Practice to Mastery

The basic plan of Active Learning is for you to help your teen recognize and overcome or eliminate barriers that keep her from working up to her full potential in school. As you do that, the first tangible result will be her increased willingness and success in doing homework. Through her homework she will learn more, participate more effectively in class, score higher on tests, and get higher grades. All of those results will make her happy and proud, increasing her motivation for school. Her self-confidence and self-esteem will grow. She will view herself as more capable and more intelligent. Those changes will make it easier for you to relax, knowing that she is responsibly preparing herself for adulthood. As you more comfortably accept her increasing independence, there will be fewer arguments and less defiance.

So that's the general outline of where we are headed: namely, toward getting your teen to do her homework regularly and completely. Of course, you've been working at that for years. But if your family is at all like most of the thousands of families we've worked with, you'll find the Active Learning approach more effective and more pleasant than what you have been doing. Active Learning provides a number of specific techniques and examples of what to do. But it also introduces a general way of looking at teen and school issues that will enable you to handle the variety of individual situations that will arise with your teen.

There are some things about learning you should know in order to better understand what your teen is facing and to give her better advice when she needs it. This information is presented first to give you background on how your teen's barriers arose in the first place and why she needs your help in overcoming them. In later chapters we'll address specifically how you can help your teen lower the barriers, opening her to advice from you and others about improved learning techniques.

Learn by Doing

Perhaps the key idea to overcoming the barriers to effective learning and success in school is this: *The only way to learn anything is by practicing*. It is easy to see that practice is essential for learning skills like bicycling and piano playing. But what about education and knowledge? Does one learn all information, as well as how to think, by practicing? The answer is *yes!*

This principle—learning by doing—applies to all subjects. You learn to solve algebra problems by solving problems. You learn to write essays by writing essays. You memorize by reciting over and over. You learn to think and analyze by participating in discussions and by presenting your thoughts orally or in writing.

Are there exceptions? For example, you might ask, "Don't people learn some things by being taught, by just watching and listening?" It seems that even where there is no physical activity, learning requires mental practice. Our brains can repeat, analyze, and visualize information, helping us to remember, understand, and learn. This may explain why being engaged in listening is so much more effective than just hearing information.

Let's suppose you are watching a Little League baseball game. The players are eleven and twelve years old, and some are just beginning to mature. Marty, the pitcher for the Tigers, is within the age limit, but he looks much older than the others, bigger and better coordinated. He is dominating the game, striking out almost everyone with his curveball. The players on the Giants team would all like to get hits, so their motivation is in place. But they are not yet skillful enough to hit curveballs. They need more practice. Some of the players will practice and some won't.

Each of the Giants dealt with his disappointment and embarrassment after striking out in different ways. Charlie blamed the umpire: "At least two of those strikes he called were balls. I was robbed." Joey did some clowning around. Suzie, one of two girls on the team, thought maybe the time had come when she could no longer keep up with the boys. Fred said defensively, "Baseball's a dumb game. Who cares who wins?" He stopped showing up at games. Mel couldn't hold back the tears. Cy looked at his teammates on the bench and answered their unspoken criticism angrily: "Well, you guys didn't do any better."

Though most of the players knew they would need more practice to learn to hit curves, they also felt discouraged. They thought they couldn't keep up with pitchers like Marty: "By the time I learn to hit the pitches I faced today, Marty will still strike me out because he'll have improved more than I have." Those boys decided baseball wasn't their game.

Two of the players, encouraged by their earlier successes in other games, resolved to practice and improve. They knew their chances of reaching the major leagues, even Marty's chances, were practically zero. But they had enough pride and pleasure from their experiences to press on, to do the work of practicing in order to improve.

Though this example is from sports rather than school, you can certainly see that the barriers to practicing—to learning by doing—were primarily related to embarrassment or discouragement. It is interesting to note also that the players camouflaged those feelings in different ways. You can see that the players' parents could best help by being understanding and supportive, rather than by offering advice or rewards and punishments. So despite the importance of practice to learning, our approach will not be to force teens to practice. Rather, we will attempt to guide them toward identifying and overcoming the barriers of frustration, discouragement, embarrassment, and resistance that stand in the way of their doing the necessary work of practice.

Here is an academic example of this important point. Ted was barely passing pre-algebra. He found it difficult, not at all like the easy time he had had earlier in arithmetic. If Ted could do the homework problems, he'd breeze through them and feel fine. But if he got stuck, he felt frustrated. He'd say things like "I can't learn this. There must be something wrong with me." And he made defensive remarks like "Algebra is tough. It's irrelevant. The teacher is no good. Besides, I don't like algebra. None of the adults I know can do algebra and they're doing all right. Besides, my parents never did well in math, either."

In the Active Learning program the next summer, Ted embraced the idea of learning by practicing. So as he started algebra in the fall, he was able to look at the homework the way an athlete might view a strenuous workout. In other words, it was hard work, but it was building up his mental muscles. That insight, and the encouragement of his parents, enabled Ted to do the work. It took until March before Ted got the excited feeling that he was actually "good at math." After that he found math easy and fun. He became so good, his subsequent teachers often praised what they considered his natural aptitude.

The Importance of Homework

When we think about school courses, most of us picture a teacher lecturing in a classroom, with the students listening and taking notes. From that view, school is a kind of intelligence contest. All the students are given the same instruction and then tested to see who is smartest.

Under these conditions, some students will do better and others worse than average. And that corresponds to the usual notions about intelligence: namely, those who are intelligent in a subject learn it quickly and remember it well, and vice versa.

But that picture of school and learning totally ignores the importance of practice. For regardless of intelligence or natural ability, students who practice more perform better. Without practice, no one can become skillful at algebra problems or essay writing. Of course, the progress each student makes for each hour of practice depends on a combination of ability, interests, and prior learning. In addition, after a great deal of practice, some individuals will be much more skillful than others. The accomplishments of Newton, Mozart, and Shakespeare were not simply a matter of practice. So what we generally think of as intelligence does make some difference. But in terms of learning the material in high school and college, the students who do best have generally gotten the most practice. Sometimes they did a lot of practice last year, so they can learn the new material almost effortlessly. Also, some students do a lot of mental practice in class. We say they are paying attention. But it's more than that. They are actually repeating, analyzing, and rehearsing in their minds while listening in class.

Though more learning takes place while doing homework than while listening in class, many students think the opposite. That impression starts in the primary grades where there is little or no homework—most of the practice and learning are done in class. In contrast, colleges expect students to do two hours of homework for every hour in class. The situation in high school is in between. High schools generally have six hours in school and about two hours of homework.

During the six hours of the school day, students spend almost all of their time listening, either to teachers or to other students reciting. In class there is little or no time for practicing, for learning by doing. That is why two hours of homework is so critical. Homework is the daily exercise—the mental calisthenics—by which one learns both the content of the courses and the study habits and self-control for doing mental work.

But not having recognized this, many teens view homework as an intrusion on their own time, almost a punishment. Many teachers count homework in computing course grades, and students recognize that doing the homework will improve their learning and test scores. Still, possibly because school lasts six hours and homework just two hours, many students think of homework as an optional extra, something mainly for nerds. Many believe the brightest students earn A's without studying, doing only the required homework effortlessly and quickly. In addition, of course, homework has to compete with the teen's social life and recreation. And finally, in doing homework, the teen will often be confronting the three barriers we identified in the last chapter:

- Resistance: The teen may resist or rebel in an unskillful attempt to get different treatment from her parents or teachers.
- Study skills: The teen may not know how to go about studying and learning the assignment.
- Self-confidence: Because she doesn't expect to succeed, the teen may not believe her efforts will be worthwhile.

Homework Is Done at Home

Intuitively, parents know that homework is important. In addition, it is supposed to be done at home, where we have at least the possibility of directing our teens. So when parents take an active role in their teens' educations, most of their actions are directed at homework. That emphasis is appropriate; homework is crucial. What your teen does about homework largely determines everything else in her education.

Teachers try all sorts of things to get teens to do their homework. They count the homework in calculating grades. Some teachers give extra credit for homework. Others will flunk students who miss more than a few assignments. Many teachers spend hours at home correcting and grading homework. Helpful as those actions are, they do not address the three barriers that are standing in the way of so many students.

Is the Homework the Right Practice?

Obviously, to learn correctly you have to practice correctly. In fact, you learn what you practice. If you practice in the wrong way, you may develop wrong ideas or bad habits that are difficult to unlearn. So a student should practice doing exactly what he is trying to learn to do.

Generally the assignments in school provide that practice. If the students are going to be tested and graded on translating from Spanish to English, the teacher will usually assign similar translations as homework. But sometimes teachers don't do that.

In Roger's history course, the homework assignments were to read (or study) the textbook, but the tests included essay questions. Roger did his homework regularly, reading the assigned chapters and highlighting important points. He also paid attention in class and took notes. Before the first two exams, he reviewed his notes and the points he had highlighted in the text. He even spent time memorizing key names, dates, and places. But his exam scores were barely passing. When he expressed his frustration to his mom, she acknowledged all the effort he had put out. Then, when he said "I don't know what to do," she saw an opening to give some advice. She suggested he allocate fifty minutes to giving himself a practice test with three essay questions, as though he were taking the test. For his practice test, Roger selected three essay questions from the textbook. By practicing in that way, he became more aware of what he didn't need to memorize and of how to interpret and present key ideas. His grades went up and he started liking history.

Here's another example. For the first quarter, Laura got four A's and a D in Spanish. The homework in Spanish, which she did thoroughly, consisted of the usual reading and writing exercises, with about fifteen new vocabulary words per week. But each Friday the instructor gave a quiz, and those quizzes were defeating Laura. On each quiz the instructor played a tape of a person telling a little story in Spanish. At the end of the story, the narrator would ask questions about the story and the students were to write their answers to the questions in Spanish. Laura was having difficulty understanding the story and the questions.

When I talked with Laura and got this background information, I suggested that she arrange to practice listening to spoken Spanish. She and her mother went to a bookstore and bought some Spanish tapes (not the same tapes the instructor used in class). Laura listened to her tapes less than an hour per week, but that made all the difference for her.

Learning to speak and understand spoken language are separate skills and each can be learned only if it is practiced specifically. But since speaking a foreign language is so appealing, students often enjoy and are motivated by practicing speaking and understanding, even if they are not graded on those skills.

Math courses confuse many students because math courses require three different kinds of practice. First, there are facts—formulas and definitions—to be memorized. Then there are techniques and methods to be learned by practice, such as simplifying expressions. Finally, there are problems to solve, which requires its own special kind of practice. For problem solving, the real issue is how to start—that is, how to choose the right method. This step is so obvious to experts that they may have difficulty explaining how they know that one method is more appropriate than some other method.

For the beginner, the way to develop that ability is by practice. The right practice would go something like this: As the student completes each chapter in the textbook, she should write some typical problems from that chapter on three-by-five-inch cards. Because a problem comes from a particular chapter, it is clear that the right method for that problem is one of the methods covered in that chapter. So the student can write the name of the appropriate method on the back of each card. The practice then involves looking at the problem and trying to name the method to use. Students who make a deck of such flashcards and do this sort of drill throughout the semester soon unlock the mysteries of math. (Also, see the special note about algebra in the appendix.)

Another situation in which the homework doesn't provide the practice a student needs is where the student is supposed to already possess certain skills but doesn't.

This issue of prerequisites is very important and will be discussed later.

Mastery Learning

We have talked about the importance of practice and the need to do the right kinds of practice. Now let's consider how much practice it takes. The answer is to practice to mastery—practicing one skill or assignment to mastery before going on to the next level. Though that might initially take a little extra time, as you master each step along the way, the next steps go faster and more easily. So overall you save time. A graph of mastery learning looks like this:

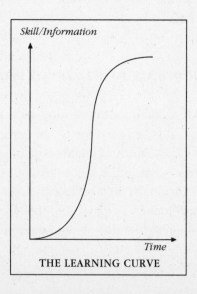

Skill/Information

Time

THE LEARNING CURVE

Think about children in first grade on the day the class has completed addition and is starting subtraction. Since they have learned to add, they are moving along the learning curve a little faster than before. So the curve turns up. But suppose Betty has not yet mastered adding. She is going to need more time to learn subtraction than everyone else. Therefore she is likely to fall even farther behind.

As a student begins falling behind in a course, she needs more time than everyone else to do the current work, plus she needs time to catch up. In addition, there's the emotional impact: that sinking feeling of discouragement. Most of us can recall falling behind in a course. Maybe we passed, but we may never have gotten rid of the feeling that we couldn't succeed in that field. And since then we have probably avoided courses or careers that involved that subject.

The Elements of Mastery Learning

To better understand mastery learning and to guide your teen in using it, it is helpful to break the learning process into specific steps. These steps are only one way of describing mastery learning, and at times the steps may be combined or arranged in a different order. Still, they provide a convenient way to present the key points. The six basic elements of mastery learning are as follows.

Goals

In mastery learning your teenager will keep working until she masters or achieves the next goal. So the goal needs to be clear and attainable in the next few hours or days. Larger, long-term goals must be broken down into smaller steps to define what is to be worked on and mastered today. For each assignment, your teen needs a sufficiently clear idea of what is to be learned so that she can tell whether she has in fact reached that goal. With a little practice, this is really quite simple. Generally teachers provide this information, though students frequently ignore it. The goal should be stated in terms of the skills or knowledge to be learned, rather than in terms of time or number of problems to be done.

For example, suppose the immediate goal in an algebra class is to learn to use the quadratic formula. Toward that goal the algebra teacher gives an assignment of ten problems. Presumably, if your teen does the ten problems, she will know how to use the formula. But suppose she gets help on the first three problems in class, the next four are particularly easy, and she gets the last three wrong. She's done ten problems, but she hasn't mastered the material.

Preparation

To become good at anything, your teenager needs to practice. But before she can begin to practice, she needs some *preparation*, some information or a demonstration about what and how to practice. She might get that information by listening in class, by reading, or by watching a film. Most of what happens in high-school and college classes is preparation, not practice. Usually the practice is done at home or in the library or study hall.

For example, the teacher in an English class can describe how to do a book report, and perhaps will hand out an excellent book report as an example. But none of that is practice. It is preparation for the actual practice of writing a book report.

Practice

Your teen will learn by practicing. Ideally, she will practice to mastery. The amount of practice she needs to reach mastery may be more or less than others need and may be different than you or she expected.

It is useful to note the difference between practice and tests. A football team is judged by how many points they can score in sixty minutes of play. That's the test. They are not judged by how many hours of practice it took them, individually or collectively, to develop their skills. The same idea applies to homework. Within some limits, your teen can devote additional time to master assignments. Knowing about the learning curve may help her realize the extra effort will soon pay off. On the other hand, if she lacks the prerequisites or falls behind during the semester, it may become impossible for her to keep up. If a student falls a month behind in a course, she probably will not be able to catch up.

Feedback

Feedback lets your teen know whether she has practiced to mastery. Feedback will also let her know whether she is doing the right kind of practice and doing it efficiently. Some examples of feedback are test scores and teachers' comments on homework. As your teen practices using mastery learning, she will get better at providing her own feedback. Getting her started is covered in later chapters.

Resources

Resources are the materials and people needed to succeed in a course. This includes the obvious resources like the teacher, the classroom, and notebook paper. In addition, your teen may need various supplies, references, and human helpers to master her courses. Initially you may need to help her identify and gather the necessary resources. In time, your teen should be doing this on her own.

Prerequisites

You and your teen should consider the prerequisites for each of her courses. Consider all of the skills and knowledge she should have at the beginning of her courses for each semester. Obviously, being able to read and write is a prerequisite for high-school courses. But in addition, students may be expected to already have mastery of note-taking, writing essays, memorizing, or fractions.

Benefits of Mastery Learning

Initially, mastery learning may take extra time and effort, but there are big payoffs in addition to having a faster learning rate. First, skills we have mastered will stay with us longer. Once you have learned to ride a bicycle, you never forget. Contrast that to what happens in algebra. Most of us passed algebra in high school without mastering it. By the time we graduated from high school, most of us totally forgot algebra. The same was true of foreign languages, history, and biology. By not taking our skills to mastery, we lost most of the benefit of the time and effort we put into passing those courses.

Another dividend of mastery learning comes from setting goals for each assignment and then achieving those goals. This provides a satisfying sense of accomplishment and completion. If you aren't aware of progress, a task can seem like endless drudgery. By eliminating that feeling and replacing it with feelings of success, mastery learning helps students like school better.

As a student begins to master assignments and succeed in learning the subjects, she becomes willing and able to take responsibility for her own learning. Students who are mastering their courses begin to see teachers as helpers rather than as opponents. They are able to focus on the work, getting as much help as possible from the teacher. Finally, mastering a subject builds self-esteem and confidence. Notice that someone who learns a subject quickly and remembers it is considered smart in that subject. Interesting, isn't it? Mastery learning makes a student feel smart and appear smart to others.

A conversation I had with a young man named Shawn illustrates the power of both the techniques of mastery learning and the way in which the idea of mastery learning helps students overcome feelings of inadequacy. Shawn had been a mediocre high-school student and had dropped or flunked all of the courses in his first year at a community college. At his mother's urging, he had enrolled in Active Learning. Though he said he learned useful study skills, he still said, "I'd like to be a psychologist, but college just isn't for me. So I'm leaving school and going to work."

I asked Shawn what he liked to do and what he was good at. He said that in sharp contrast to school, he had always liked and been very good at sports, especially baseball. I said I was sure he had practiced more—hit more pitches and fielded more grounders—than the other kids on his Little League team. At first he said no. Then, as he thought about it, he remembered practicing more regularly, staying more hours, and getting more innings of play than his teammates. He next said that though he had probably practiced more, it had always seemed easy because of his natural ability. To some extent he was certainly right. But it also must have seemed easy because he was meeting or exceeding his own and his coaches' and parents' expectations.

Then Shawn told me about learning to pitch a curveball. He had seen it done and had been shown how, but he couldn't do it. He said, "I practiced every day for weeks, throwing pitch after pitch, and still it wouldn't curve. I decided to keep trying no matter what. I just worked and worked and worked. Finally, after three months, practically at the end of the summer, I got it."

At that point Shawn stopped talking for a reflective moment, and then he said, "I'm going back to college this fall."

Using Mastery Learning in Regular Courses

Lots of research has been done on having teachers run their classes on the basis of mastery learning. The results are unclear. The big problem is that students take different amounts of time to master their lessons. How is a teacher to run the classroom and teach the lesson with everyone moving at different speeds? Many approaches have been tried, sometimes with very positive results. But most teachers and administrators have decided mastery learning is unworkable as the basis for running classes and schools.

On the other hand, within some limits, students have the time they need to master their homework assignments. So they can use mastery learning at home, even though their classes operate in the usual way. This idea can help you guide and advise your teen in handling homework.

If She Hasn't Mastered the Prerequisites

Barely passing a prerequisite course is not enough. For example, a student should have mastered Spanish I before starting Spanish II. In other words, on the first day of Spanish II, she should be able to score at least a B on the final exam for Spanish I. Having gotten a C or D—or maybe even a B—months earlier means she is starting at a disadvantage.

If a student doesn't have the prerequisites for a course, there are really only three choices:

1. Postpone this course until she has mastered the prerequisites.
2. Put in an enormous effort at the beginning to catch up.
3. Accept the likelihood of having great difficulty in the course and doing poorly.

Usually it is best to postpone the course. Even if a student knows going in that she is taking on an extra challenge, catching up on prerequisites while keeping up with the present course is very tough.

Postponing a high-school course is highly unusual and may strike you as unrealistic. After all, the four-year curriculum seems fairly inflexible, especially for students preparing for college. It may seem your teen has to take an English course every semester, has to finish algebra in ninth grade and geometry the year after, and so on. Though the majority of college students at some colleges now take five years to get their bachelor's degrees, a fifth year of high school is very unusual and probably not a realistic option. So my advice about postponing courses may seem extreme. But even with all these constraints, it is possible to postpone courses and still graduate and get admitted to college on time.

Summer school provides one alternative for your teen to repeat a course or to make up time if she repeats a course during the school year. But even without summer school, there is some flexibility to rearrange your teen's courses, and the advantages of taking time to master the prerequisites are great. Rarely will a student with good grades be denied college admissions because she lacks some course. Much more frequently, students who could easily have excelled in high school fall behind, get discouraged, and give up on higher education.

Tutoring can sometimes be used to allow your teen to make up prerequisites while taking the usual college preparatory classes on the usual schedule. But be cautious. Remember that until a student has mastered the prerequisites, she will be having added difficulty with the current courses, on top of the extra time with the tutor on those prerequisites. So only a limited amount of catch-up can be done during a semester, and it generally needs to happen right away.

The basic prerequisites for high school are reading, writing, and math. If you are not certain your teen can read at her grade level, with a speed of at least two hundred words per minute, it is worth finding out. If you call her high-school counselor, the counselor should be able to look in your teen's file and tell you her reading level, as measured on a standardized test. If your teen hasn't been tested in several years or there is any doubt about her reading skills, there is a quick test included in the appendix that you can use to find out how well she reads.

Your teen should be able to write sensible, grammatical paragraphs and essays. If not, she should take English classes in which she can successfully advance from where she is to mastery at the high-school level. If you are in doubt about her writing ability, read her papers and confer with her teachers. Without the ability to write excellent essays at the high-school level, she will be unable to succeed in courses involving compositions, written reports, essay exams, or term papers. So she may struggle in courses such as history for want of writing skills that are not taught in the course.

The prerequisites for high-school math are a major problem. You see, knowing fractions is an absolute prerequisite for algebra and for chemistry and physics. This is definite. Trying to learn algebra without knowing fractions is as difficult as trying to learn from a book without knowing how to read. It just can't be done. Despite this, most students enter algebra without having mastered fractions. When these students flounder in algebra, they and others incorrectly blame their IQ, motivation, or aptitude for math. Do not let your teen start algebra without being able to calculate with fractions. That includes being able to add, subtract, multiply, divide, and simplify fractions. If you can't make up a test on your own, get any sixth-, seventh-, or eighth-grade math textbook or workbook with answers and use the problems in it as a test.

You don't have to worry about assessing grade level or IQ. Your teen either knows how to calculate with fractions or she doesn't. If she doesn't, she needs to learn how. Learning fractions may take a ninth grader perhaps eight hours of diligent work. Since the time is relatively short, it may seem that the need is not crucial. But proceeding without it is like driving your car without oil in the engine.

A lack of a prerequisite skill does not indicate a learning disability, or the need for special education classes. It just means that for some reason, somewhere along the line, your teen did not master that skill or has forgotten it.

To learn a prerequisite skill, your teen may need to take a special course, get some tutoring, or study on her own. Whatever it will take, this effort may be even more unappealing to her than her regular schoolwork. This is because it may seem like extra and unnecessary work, and because she will almost certainly be embarrassed and pained about needing what she considers remedial tutoring. So if your teen needs remedial work, the Active Learning approaches presented in succeeding chapters will be especially useful to you in helping her do what is needed.

The Role of Teachers and Teaching

With all of this emphasis on learning by doing and practicing to mastery, students can still learn from teachers. One of a teacher's most important functions is to show students how to practice and give them assignments. The teacher may demonstrate and explain how to solve a problem, or discuss how to analyze a novel. Then the teacher gives assignments; perhaps parts are to be done in class, the rest is assigned as homework. The teacher also manages group practice activities such as class discussions, and provides guidance and encouragement, complimenting good work, correcting mistakes, and encouraging the students to do enough practice. Finally, teachers evaluate and grade the students.

Note that this summary of the important and useful activities of teachers does not include lecturing. Though lecture has a definite place in teaching and learning, there is too much of it in most classrooms. Many approaches to improving schools are based on replacing some of the time spent listening to lectures with other activities. Since the invention of the printing press made books the most efficient way to transmit most information, the primary value of lecture has been to expose students to the personalities of their professors and teachers. Teachers provide role models, inspiring students to select certain fields of study and careers. So while too much lecturing is the general rule, teachers have a role as lecturers, too.

Thus we see that even though students learn mainly through the practice they do at home, their teachers can and should play a significant role in learning.

So Far, So Good

Now that you understand all these fine ideas about learning, you may be wondering how you get your teen to understand and act accordingly. Well, we're coming to that. In the next chapter we'll discuss your overall role in your teen's education. Then subsequent chapters will cover the details on how to proceed.

Chapter 2 Key Points

1. All learning is achieved by practicing. There are only a few minutes of practice in a typical school day. That is why homework is crucial.
2. Mastery learning is practicing the present assignment until you have mastered it.
3. Your teen can apply mastery learning even though the teachers run their classes in the usual way.
4. Mastery learning involves:
   a. Having a clearly defined goal
   b. Preparing to practice, in class or by studying
   c. Practicing
   d. Getting feedback
5. The benefits of mastery learning are:
   a. Your teen's learning rate accelerates.
   b. Later lessons and subjects will be easier.
   c. Teens remember things longer.
   d. Teens feel successful along the way.
   e. Teens are aware of making progress.

Chapter 3

Reducing Resistance

The three barriers to success in school are resistance, a lack of learning skills, and a lack of self-confidence as a student. For parents of teens, the best starting place in overcoming those barriers is to work on eliminating resistance. Once you have helped him to reduce if not eliminate any resistance, your teen will be able to build and use his learning skills to improve his school performance. As he does that, his self-confidence and motivation as a student will increase. Then, as he has more success, you and he will be able to make additional progress on lowering and then removing any remaining resistance he may have that blocks his path to success.

This chapter provides the general approach for parents in lowering teenage resistance. The subsequent chapters provide specific tools and examples to put this approach into practice.

Your Teen Still Needs You

Even more powerful than peer pressure is a teen's need to feel love, acceptance, and admiration from his parents. Teens also need to learn to be independent and self-reliant. These two needs are not exactly opposites, but they are often difficult to balance. So it is not surprising that teens are not always successful in getting those needs met. In an ideal situation, the teen handles some area of his life, such as homework, responsibly. As a consequence of that, his parents express confidence in his self-management and allow him almost complete independence in that area. The teen feels independent and admirable and lovable. This is the kind of "success breeds success" situation we want.

But teens often get off track and do things that are unsuccessful, counterproductive, and even self-damaging. They lose or forget to hand in completed homework; they forget about or neglect to do assignments and chores; they argue or refuse to talk. In short, they do all sorts of infuriating, seemingly irrational things. But all behavior is purposeful. So no matter how unsuccessful and unskillful those behaviors may seem, they are actually the teen's way of trying to meet his need to feel lovable and independent.

This can help us understand why some teens act so defiant, hostile, or sullen toward their parents. If a teen does things to please his parents, he will be giving up his independence. But if he proceeds too independently, he may cut off the emotional and material support he still needs. Caught in this double bind, teens get confused. They may do something positive but complain or act surly to salvage a feeling of independence. Or they may consciously or unconsciously do negative things to prove their independence to us and to themselves.

This negative situation can start quite accidentally and persist until you recognize it and take action to correct it. For example, to assist our teens in school and in life, we parents give our teens a lot of advice and constructive criticism. But on the receiving end, this is a double whammy. First, they are being criticized, so maybe they are not lovable. And second, we are still trying to limit their independence. So even seemingly innocent attempts to strike up a conversation with our teens—such as the question "How did you do on that test today?"—can cause a teen a surprising amount of pain. In response, he may be actively or passively rebellious, often without being conscious of why. This chapter presents a model of the teen years that you will find helpful in reversing or avoiding such negative interactions.

A Time of Transition

In the teen years your child has to learn to manage all areas of his own life. Of course, to learn he has to practice. And until he has practiced to mastery in any area, you both must expect he's going to make some mistakes. By viewing mistakes as an inevitable part of practicing and learning, you will stay calmer and make better decisions about how to correct and protect him.

Over the years you will delegate more and more control to your teen so he can practice managing his own life. What you continue to control and what you delegate to your teen requires continuous and rapid adjustment. Making those decisions is both difficult and frightening. It's difficult because neither you nor he knows for sure when he is ready to handle any particular aspect of his life. It is frightening because you want to protect him from getting hurt by his mistakes. Disagreements on these issues are natural and are the source of many conflicts between parents and teens. Parents are like a driving instructor in a dual-control car. The student is driving most of the time, but the instructor is there to keep him from crashing.

When Paul entered high school, his parents felt he became very uncooperative, almost defiant. They worried that he was not doing well in his studies, was hanging around with the wrong friends, was forgetful about his chores, and was moody. He complained that they were too controlling.

Using the Active Learning approach, Paul's parents got together with him to talk over the situation. They all agreed that Paul had to attend school without cutting. He could choose his own friends. He could come and go as he wished, as long as he was home by ten P.M. on weekdays and eleven-thirty P.M. on Friday and Saturday. Also, he was to tell his parents where he was going and who he was with. Paul could manage his own homework, but he was expected to do all of it and to get at least B grades. They also agreed to meet weekly to see how this arrangement was working. Things improved a lot.

As Paul got older, they relaxed his curfew. When Paul started dating and spent hours on the phone each evening, his grades fell. He and his parents talked it over. He said he was too old to be told when he could or couldn't talk on the phone. They said he was neglecting his schoolwork, so maybe they should increase his motivation by restricting his phone use. When the smoke cleared, they agreed that Paul would not take calls or make calls from seven to nine each evening. That would assure two hours of uninterrupted time for his work. After a few months, Paul had a steady girlfriend and they usually studied together at his house or hers. So the telephone problem went away.

Still later, Paul started smoking and wanted to get a car. He and his parents made some new agreements. He was not to smoke in the house (and they hoped he would quit altogether). He could share the use of the two family cars with his parents, but he would have to pay for the increased cost of insurance by working during vacations and on weekends.

As you can see from this example, Paul and his parents kept changing the rules as appropriate to Paul's age and experience. We can see in the situations involving friends, homework, a steady girlfriend, and smoking that his parents allowed him to make many of his own decisions. At least with the smoking it is clear that Paul made a poor choice, one with potentially important and long-term negative consequences. But his parents decided—wisely, I think—to express their hopes and leave control with Paul.

Do I Let Go Now?

When you helped your child learn to ride a two-wheeled bike, you held the seat to keep him from falling and getting hurt. At the point when you are just about to let go, some children are saying, "Don't let go. Don't let go." Others think they can handle it on their own and say, "Let go. Let go. I can do it." In either case, the child's level of confidence may or may not match his actual skill. But knowing how he feels at the moment will help you make your decision about letting go.

To handle your role as parent, *you need to know what's happening*—you need details about how your teen is doing and what he is thinking. Just as in teaching bike riding, you need to observe how well he is riding and to hear from him how well he thinks he is riding. With that information, you are in a position to make your decisions about when to let go.

Where Does Your Teenager Stand Now?

Before trying to improve how your teen does in school and how you get along together at home, take stock of how things are now. This will help you identify where to start and will also provide you with a baseline against which to measure progress. Being aware of any improvements lets you and your teen know you are going in the right direction and derive satisfaction and motivation from your accomplishments.

Questionnaire

Take a few minutes now to fill out this questionnaire about how things are now for your teenager. This will help you identify what is working, set goals for improvements, and be aware of progress. For each item, check the frequency with which your teen does this. Then check your rating of his performance of this item.

	Frequency				**Rating**		
	Never	Seldom	Usually	Always	Out-standing	Satis-factory	Needs improvement
In School							
Attends classes	☐	☐	☐	☐	☐	☐	☐
Knows what is required	☐	☐	☐	☐	☐	☐	☐
Participates in class	☐	☐	☐	☐	☐	☐	☐
Gets along with teachers	☐	☐	☐	☐	☐	☐	☐
Asks for help when needed	☐	☐	☐	☐	☐	☐	☐
Learns subjects thoroughly	☐	☐	☐	☐	☐	☐	☐
Enjoys school	☐	☐	☐	☐	☐	☐	☐
Participates in school activities	☐	☐	☐	☐	☐	☐	☐
Feels able to succeed	☐	☐	☐	☐	☐	☐	☐

	Frequency				Rating		
	Never	Seldom	Usually	Always	Outstanding	Satisfactory	Needs improvement
In Doing Homework							
Knows the assignments	☐	☐	☐	☐	☐	☐	☐
Gets started promptly	☐	☐	☐	☐	☐	☐	☐
Works steadily	☐	☐	☐	☐	☐	☐	☐
Does it well	☐	☐	☐	☐	☐	☐	☐
Turns it in on time	☐	☐	☐	☐	☐	☐	☐
Asks for help when needed	☐	☐	☐	☐	☐	☐	☐
Knows how to study for each subject	☐	☐	☐	☐	☐	☐	☐
Plans ahead for large assignments	☐	☐	☐	☐	☐	☐	☐
Manages time well	☐	☐	☐	☐	☐	☐	☐
Is well organized	☐	☐	☐	☐	☐	☐	☐
At Home							
Gets along with family	☐	☐	☐	☐	☐	☐	☐
Talks things over with parents	☐	☐	☐	☐	☐	☐	☐
Tells the truth	☐	☐	☐	☐	☐	☐	☐
Enjoys friends	☐	☐	☐	☐	☐	☐	☐
Enjoys recreational activities	☐	☐	☐	☐	☐	☐	☐
Sets goals	☐	☐	☐	☐	☐	☐	☐
Achieves his goals	☐	☐	☐	☐	☐	☐	☐
Does his chores	☐	☐	☐	☐	☐	☐	☐
Behaves responsibly	☐	☐	☐	☐	☐	☐	☐
Has a job	☐	☐	☐	☐	☐	☐	☐
Feels successful	☐	☐	☐	☐	☐	☐	☐

If you didn't rate your teen as satisfactory in many areas and outstanding in at least a few, your teen almost certainly feels that you do not approve of him. We'll approach that issue in a moment.

Now, before going on, based on the questionnaire you should select one, two, or at most three issues to work on with your teen. You can't work on everything at once, and once things begin to improve in one or two areas, everything else will get better more easily, maybe even effortlessly. If you have just one or two areas that need improvement, the choices are obvious. But if you'd like to see improvement in five or ten or even twenty-five areas, you'll have to be selective. Choose the areas that seem as though they are crucial and that might possibly be cleared up in a week or two. Save long-range issues for later. For example, "Attends classes" is a more workable first step than "Feels able to succeed" or "Enjoys school." Don't start to work on these issues yet. But as you read, you may want to think about how the general advice and examples apply to your teen and the issues you would like to approach first.

Competition out There, Compassion at Home

If schools operated on a mastery learning model—if they were set up for getting every student to master all the material and skills in the curriculum—almost all students would do better, like school more, and feel better about themselves. Whether or not this will, can, or should happen, it can't happen in time for your teen. For better or worse, intentionally or unintentionally, most schools foster a sense of competition among students to earn grades and opportunities for the future. And to repeat what has been said before, that competition leaves most students with a low opinion of their own intellectual and academic abilities.

Academically, socially, and personally, teens live in a challenging and competitive world. They need and want their parents on their side. So let the outside world provide the challenge and criticism. You need to provide love, acceptance, empathy, and assistance.

The Paradox of High Expectations and Lots of Encouragement

When a student is a beginner in a field, parents and teachers need to be very supportive and encouraging. A beginner's self-confidence is low and fragile. He can't tolerate much criticism, no matter how constructive it may be. When a child in preschool draws a picture, we praise it and the child. No matter what a preschooler's drawing looks like, we say, "That's great. I really like the colors you used. I'm going to put this on the refrigerator door so I can enjoy it all the time." Even hinting that the beginner's progress should be faster may convince him this field is not for him. He may decide his natural ability is too low to make it worth doing all the practice needed to improve and ultimately excel.

On the other hand, as parents we want to assist our teens in achieving all they can. Doesn't this mean we need to have high expectations? Shouldn't we hold them to high standards of achievement, to encourage our children to be the best they can be? In contrast to *Romper Room*–style praise, shouldn't we use the Vince Lombardi approach? Vince Lombardi was the football coach who is legendary for having said "Winning isn't everything, it's the only thing."

The answer to this dilemma is to realize your teen is on his own learning curve in each subject or area of life. In some areas he is a beginner and in other areas an expert. Without lowering your ultimate hopes and expectations for your teen, the next step must always be based on where he is now. Build the experience of success. Whatever your teen's current level of school performance and responsibility are, aim for a small improvement each week. Small improvements and successes add up to major ones.

Bob Trait's parents were sure that Bob was capable of straight A's but he was getting mostly B's and a few C's. He wasn't a difficult child at home or at school, but he put out only a minimal effort in his studies. At report card time, their conversations were something like this:

MR. TRAIT: Bob, these are pretty good grades, but I feel you could get A's with just a little bit more effort.

BOB: My grades are all right. In fact, they're better than most of my friends'. I don't see why you are unhappy with how I'm doing.

In response, Mr. Trait always tried calmly and patiently to convince Bob that he could do better, that it would take very little more effort, and that the payoffs would be very worthwhile. And Bob always got angry and impatient, sometimes arguing back and other times refusing to talk. Mr. Trait just couldn't understand Bob's annoyance and resistance.

When I suggested that the Traits focus on Bob's achievements rather than shortcomings, they understood the idea but were not convinced it would work. Mr. Trait said, "We have to stay on Bob every day just to get him to do the minimum. If we let up at all, won't he do even less and get worse grades?"

But following my suggestion, the Traits sat down right there and told Bob that they realized he was doing much better than average in school and that they loved him and were pleased that he was so bright and capable. They didn't add that they felt frustrated that he was not working up to his potential. The end of the story is Bob began to take charge of himself and became an almost straight-A student.

Just to avoid any possible misunderstanding, being a loving and supportive parent does not mean being overly permissive. Permissiveness means accepting negative and unsuccessful actions as the equals of positive and successful actions. That's not the idea. What we're after is accepting our teens as they are *and* helping them develop positive attitudes, skills, and habits.

200 Percent Responsibility

You want your teen to be 100 percent responsible for his own education. But you obviously have a role, too. So do you divide the responsibility, starting at 95 percent for you and 5 percent for him, and working toward zero for you? No. You are 100 percent responsible for your role, and he is 100 percent responsible for his. That's 200 percent responsibility, which may surprise you. But at work, the manager is 100 percent responsible for getting the job done. Then the supervisors are 100 percent responsible for their departments. And finally, each employee is 100 percent responsible for his or her assigned tasks. Unlike control or authority or money, responsibility isn't limited to 100 percent. In the family, parents and teen are each responsible for different tasks, and those tasks change over time.

When talking about school, parents sometimes speak as though they are in school, too. They say things like "We're not doing too well in algebra. We got a C-minus. It looks like we'll be going to summer school." I used to hesitate making a point of this, but I now think it is worth paying attention to. If you have been talking like that, switch your thinking and your words to match the real responsibilities. You are responsible for assisting, guiding, and encouraging, but your teen is responsible for doing the work of practicing and learning. The learning and the grades are his. There will be more discussion and specific examples later concerning who is responsible for what. For now, just be aware that you shouldn't take on his responsibilities, nor should you abdicate your own.

Do You Love Me?

No matter what teens say or do, they want to feel worthy of their parents' love, respect, and admiration. Well, you certainly love your children and would do anything you could to protect and care for them. If you thought it necessary, you'd even die for them.

In some ways, your teen knows you love him. But on a daily basis, teens have doubts about being lovable and need to be reassured. The same thing happens between spouses. Every couple has conversations like this:

"Do you love me?"

"Of course. You know I do."

"Well, it wouldn't hurt to say so once in a while."

Teens aren't always up to such a direct request, but the need is there. To get on a positive footing and stay there, it helps to explicitly tell your teen—by word and deed—of your basic position: namely, that you love him and will be there to assist him, no matter what happens. You might write out a Declaration of Love, like the one that follows.

This declaration of love, or something very similar, surely reflects your true feelings for your teen. But for some reason, most of us would feel awkward reading or saying these things to our teens. If you could, it would be terrific. But perhaps some alternative would feel more appropriate. You might copy or rewrite the sample declaration as a letter to your teen. Or you might photocopy or rewrite it and post it on the refrigerator.

Whether or not you do any of those things, you should reread this declaration from time to time. Especially when you are faced with an upsetting or confusing situation with your teen, this declaration can remind you of your most important goals and feelings, so you can handle day-to-day issues with greater success.

Declaration of Love

I love you. I am on your side and will always be here for you. I will do what I think best for you no matter what happens, no matter what you do.

I hope and expect that you will be self-confident, well adjusted, healthy, and successful in whatever way is appropriate for you.

I want the best for you, balancing your present well-being and happiness with adequate preparation for your future.

I am responsible for assisting you in developing into a responsible, self-reliant adult, able to handle and enjoy your own life.

We may not always agree on what is best. I will have to act according to my best judgment.

I know that you can and should take charge of more and more of your own life as you grow and mature. Neither of us can know exactly when you are capable and comfortable with handling any particular area of your life. So we will experiment together. To monitor and adjust the level and rate of my delegating control to you,

I must have information about what you think and how you are doing in all areas of your life.

Further, because of my concern for you, I am happy about your successes, distressed about your failures, and worried if I don't know what is happening. As your loving and supportive parent, I am entitled to know what is going on.

I will negotiate with you in good faith to adjust what I do and what you do so that we can both be comfortable with our mutual commitments and relationship. I will not cave in, nor do I expect you to cave in. But I expect both of us to work together to resolve any conflicts in a mutually acceptable way.

Love,
Mom/Dad

Chapter 3 Key Points

1. Teens want and need to feel worthy of your love and admiration.

2. Let your teen know, by word and deed, that you love him and will assist him, no matter what.

3. In the teen years, you delegate control piece-meal so your teen can practice taking care of himself.

4. Until your teen has mastered any area, he will make mistakes. By remembering that mistakes are an inevitable part of practicing and learning, you will stay calmer and make better decisions about how to correct and protect your teen.

5. To decide what to delegate, it helps to know what your teen knows and how confident he is. (Getting him to tell you is the subject of the next chapter.)

6. If he is a beginner in an area, be very supportive. An expert can handle more constructive criticism, but even an expert may be demoralized by too much "helpful" advice and criticism.

7. Progress toward long-range goals must be a series of small successes building from where your teen is now in each area of life. Maintain high hopes and expectations, while recognizing and appreciating one small step after another.

Chapter 4

Opening a Clear Channel of Communication

To help your teen succeed in school, you need accurate information about what is going on and what she is thinking. For example, when Sharon came home with a low grade on a math test and blamed the teacher, her mother thought the problem was that she didn't like math, procrastinated, was lazy about the homework, and had an unrealistic view of who was at fault.

In truth, the problem was something quite different. If her mother took action on those issues, she might have made matters worse. For despite those initial outbursts, it turned out Sharon was avoiding her math work because she felt hopelessly behind. She believed she was incapable of excelling in math, but she was embarrassed to tell anyone other than her friends. Even with them, she often defended herself against the pain of feeling unworthy by saying math was irrelevant and that she didn't care about school.

From what has been said so far, you can probably see

that Active Learning involves a fair amount of talking things over with your teen. For some of you this may seem natural enough. But for most parents and teens, there are certain issues that lead to arguments or silence. This chapter addresses what to do when your teen says "Haven't got time now. See you later" or "I don't want to talk about it" or retreats into her bedroom and turns up the music.

They Don't Listen

This is a common complaint of parents *and* teens. Each feels the other is being stubborn, argumentative, and un-communicative. Communication breaks down. As a result, when problems arise, we parents can't find out exactly what is wrong and what our teens think about it—information that would help us choose the right things to say and do. Nor does it seem that our teens hear what we're saying. So we lecture them repetitively or give orders that don't address the real problem. That frustrates the teens. To them, we seem out of touch and more concerned with their school grades than with their well-being.

The first goal in handling any issues with your teen is to establish open and honest communications: *Before trying to communicate anything, be sure you have an open and clear channel.*

Be a Good Listener

This chapter is about opening and maintaining a clear channel of communication with your teen. Your current communications may be excellent, or communications may be so completely broken down you can't get your teen to talk or listen to you. Your family may be between those extremes. Perhaps communications are generally good but there are certain topics you avoid or argue about.

Regardless of the present condition of the channel of communication with your teen, you will probably find the communication techniques included here very valuable. In many cases, these techniques alone produce all the results you could possibly hope for. These techniques are generally known as Active Listening or Reflective Listening.

Though Active Listening has a similar name and is part of the Active Learning approach, Active Listening is much older and was developed entirely separately and earlier by psychologist Thomas Gordon, the originator of Parent Effectiveness Training. Thomas's basic technique of Active Listening is now a part of almost all books and courses for parents and is also widely taught to adults in business. Our presentation differs from others in three ways. First, our examples emphasize school issues for teenagers. Second, we recommend overtly announcing when you start using the technique. Third, we have found that teens in general are as willing and able to learn and use Active

Listening as are parents. So once you have used the technique a couple of times, your teen may pick it up from you and try it on you. We suggest you allow and encourage your teen to use Active Listening on you.

Good communication involves both sides listening and talking. So when there's a problem or it looks like a conversation is headed toward an argument, be a good listener. The starting point for improving communications is to get your teen to talk while you listen. Getting your teen to talk—to tell you what she is really thinking—is simple, but it is not easy.

Everyone loves to talk to a good listener. A good listener is interested, understanding, and accepting of the other person and her position. A good listener is not judgmental, opinionated, or critical. She doesn't interrogate or give orders.

To get your teen to talk, be a good listener.

Active Listening

Listening is hard to do. Our attention jumps from what the speaker is saying to our own thoughts. In tense situations, instead of listening while the other person is talking, we often use the time to figure out what to say next. That means we are not focused on listening, and the speaker can sense that we're not. Then, if we disagree, argue, or criticize, she will get angry because we don't seem to have understood and considered her problems, feelings, opinions, and proposals.

Active Listening is a way of being sure you hear what the other person means, and of letting her know you have understood. In Active Listening, you listen to the other person until you think you understand her point of view. Then you check yourself by describing her point of view and asking her whether your description is correct. You actually say to the other person, "If I understand you correctly, you think _____. Is that right?" Active Listening is complete when you have described the other person's point of view to *her* satisfaction.

Here is an example. Kristi comes in after school and says, "I hate math, and I hate Mr. Flagg." An Active Listening mom would respond, "You seem really upset about math and your math teacher, Mr. Flagg." This is very likely to open the channel of communication. Kristi is likely to tell her mom more about how she feels. With more information and an open channel, her mom may be able to help in some way.

In contrast, upon hearing Kristi say she hates math and Mr. Flagg, many parents might immediately try to solve the problem. They might say "Kristi, I'm sure you would like math if you were doing better, and you could if you would just do your work regularly" or "Look, there's no point blaming Mr. Flagg for your problems in math. He offered to give you extra help but you refused to go to see him." Either of these comments—though they may be completely accurate—will tend to close down communications.

How and When to Use Active Listening

The first few times you try Active Listening, it will seem strange to you and to your teen. So before you start, announce what you are going to do and why:

> PARENT: Look, in the past when we've tried to talk about your math courses we usually got into an argument. I want to try something new. It's called Active Listening. I'm going to listen to what you have to say and then check out that I really understand your point of view. When you agree that I've heard you, I'd like you to do the same for me.

Active Listening is a tool. It is a formal, stilted way of talking. So don't try to use it for everyday conversation. When the communication is easy and open, repeating what the other person is saying is unnatural, unnecessary, and annoying. Use Active Listening for those discussions and moments when the channel of communication is closing—when one or both of you is getting angry, shouting, mumbling, or walking away.

Here's another example. A mother had often told her daughter, Jennifer, of her hopes that Jennifer would do better in school. Jennifer usually responded, "Mom, I'm just not smart enough to get A's." Then her mother would offer examples from school and elsewhere to "prove" Jennifer was smart enough to do better. That just made

Jennifer feel her mom didn't appreciate or understand her. The channel of communication between them was closed.

To open the channel, her mother needed to use Active Listening. The next time they talked, she said, "Jennifer, I've been thinking about what you said about not being smart. It must really make you feel bad, thinking you aren't smart and having Dad and me always telling you to do better in school."

This change to Active Listening was very different from what her mom had done in the past. You can understand how Jennifer would begin to feel her mom was listening rather than arguing. That would open the channel for communication. Don't worry that the mother may be reinforcing Jennifer's self-doubts. Rather, by accepting Jennifer's feelings as legitimate, without necessarily agreeing with their accuracy, the mother is likely to understand Jennifer better and to make Jennifer feel understood. This opening will help Jennifer reexamine her own thinking about her intelligence.

Accepting Versus Agreement

Using Active Listening and being empathetic doesn't mean you agree. You can be accepting of the other person and her feelings even if you think she is wrong or unreasonable. If you let her know you understand her, it opens the channel of communication. She knows you have heard her. If you still disagree at that point, it can't be because you don't care or misunderstand.

When talking to a friend, Active Listening seems very natural:

> FRIEND: God, what a day. My boss was in a terrible mood, and then two clients called up with problems. On top of that I had a headache. What a mess.
>
> YOU: Gee, I'm sorry. That sounds awful. If you want to talk, I'll listen.

Of course our friend wants to talk about it. She is upset and wants us to empathize with her. She is not ready for advice on how to fix the situation. Maybe in a few minutes or a few days she will be, but not yet.

On the other hand, with our children we tend to skip mentioning our empathy and jump right to solving the problem.

> SON: Gosh, what a day. I had a really rough exam in math and I don't think I did very well. Then my English teacher got on me about a remark I made in class. On top of that I had a headache. What a mess.

An empathetic response might be:

> PARENT: Gee, I'm sorry. That sounds awful. If you want to talk, I'll listen.

But too often, out of parental concern, we tend to say things like this:

PARENT: If you had studied last weekend like I suggested, you would have done better on that test and you wouldn't have had to stay up late last night, so you wouldn't have a headache. Now, what did you say in class that got the teacher upset?

Though this advice is well-intentioned, it closes off communication. In response, we might expect the son to say, "I don't want to talk about it."

How Much Active Listening Is Enough?

Use Active Listening until you can see and feel that the channel is open. When there's an open channel for conversation between two people, they have lots of eye contact, their body language is relaxed and attentive. They will speak in full voice. While one person is speaking, the other may be nodding, indicating the message is being received.

Some signs of a closed channel of communication are no eye contact, mumbling or no response, yelling in anger, and hostile or sullen posture. When the channel is almost completely closed, one person may turn away or retreat. If the other person reaches out a hand, the first person will probably pull away. When the channel breaks completely, one or both of them will walk away, maybe slamming the door on the way out. They will tend to avoid each other, or at least avoid talking about the subject that caused the breakdown in communication.

Do as much Active Listening as it takes to open the channel of communication. If your communications in general—or about a particular subject such as grades or homework—have been strained in the past, you may have to do a few hours of Active Listening, possibly over several days, to open the channel. Active Listening takes concentration. If you run out of energy or self-control, end the conversation and continue later.

Active Listening may seem to be time-consuming. It may seem that it would be faster if the other person would just listen carefully to what you are saying. But that's just what may have been closing off communication. So it is worth the time and effort to try to use Active Listening to resolve long-standing arguments and prevent new ones.

Use I-Messages

An I-message is one that describes how you feel or what you think. For example:

I am angry.
I feel happy.
I love you.

At first using I-messages may seem trivial, just saying something in a special way. But we know that how we talk to others—our tone and our specific words—affects the responses we get. That's why we all have spent time teaching our children to say "please" and "thank you." I-messages work at least as well as "please" and "thank you," helping you get positive responses in difficult situations.

I-messages open the channel of communication better than you-messages, suggestions, questions, and orders. Here are some examples:

I-message: I'm worried that if you watch TV, you aren't going to get your homework done.

You-message: If you are going to get your homework done, you shouldn't be watching TV.

Suggestion: You should do your homework before you watch TV.

Question: With all of the homework you have, why are you watching TV?

Order: Please turn off the TV and do your homework.

You can't use I-messages for everything you have to say. But if you are trying to open a channel of communication and keep it open, using I-messages helps. I-messages are less argumentative, less blaming, less judgmental, and more empathetic than other ways of saying the same thing. They invite dialogue and cooperation.

When you ask someone for something and she says

no, use this wonderful I-message: "I'd really like to know why." It says you are willing to listen. This is much more likely to work than asking, "Why not?"

Don't Ask

These typical parental questions usually annoy teenagers:

"What happened in school today?"
"Do you have a lot of homework tonight?"
"Have you finished your homework?"

These are perfectly reasonable questions. They are motivated by interest, concern, and a desire to help. But teens often experience questions from parents as demanding, accusing, or insulting.

So, especially if you are upset or the issue is serious, be aware that asking a question may carry extra impact that can close off communication. If possible, use I-messages to express your feelings. That is more likely to open the channel for discussing the same issues. For example, compare "Why did you get this D in math?" to "I would sure like to figure out some way for you to do better than a D in math." Here are a few more good I-messages:

"I'd love to hear about your day in school today."
"I'm not sure you've finished your homework, and I'm feeling nervous and upset."

My Teen Won't Talk

If your teen refuses to talk altogether, how can you use Active Listening? The answer is to take a guess about what your teen is saying through her nonverbal communication—her posture, expressions, and grunts.

PARENT: I'd like to talk to you about school.
TEEN: I don't have time.

The strong temptation is to just start talking—perhaps as your teen backs out of the room. Or to threaten her: "You'd better talk to me, or you won't be using the car this weekend." Instead, the Active Listening approach might be:

PARENT: It seems you don't want to talk about it.
TEEN: Well, I already know what you are going to say.
PARENT: I'd like to try to talk to you without upsetting you.

If your teen has a significant attitude problem that is a barrier to success in school, threats and demands won't get her to open up. You'll have to use Active Listening to get her to tell you about it and to let you help her deal with it.

I Feel There's Something Else

Earlier we said Active Listening is complete when the other person agrees that we have repeated back her views. But sometimes we sense she hasn't told us what is really bothering her. At that point, say something like "I feel there is something else you haven't mentioned yet."

Here's an example of a mother listening carefully to get the whole story. The mother used a Day Runner notebook to keep track of her schedule and the things she had to do. She found the notebook very useful and easy to use. But each time she suggested buying one for her son, Wayne, he stubbornly said no. That was the background when they started an Active Listening exercise in one of our programs.

MOM: Wayne, I'd like to buy you a Day Runner notebook and have you use it to keep track of your schedule and assignments.

WAYNE: No, thanks. I don't want one.

Rather than trying to persuade Wayne to use a Day Runner as she had in the past, the mother switched to Active Listening, and Wayne started to open up.

MOM: Okay. I know you don't want a Day Runner notebook. But I'd really like to know why.

WAYNE: Well, for one thing, they're expensive. And

besides, they're too big. It's not convenient to carry around another thick notebook.

MOM: So if I understand what you're saying, you don't want a Day Runner because it's expensive and a nuisance to carry around.

WAYNE: Yeah.

So far, this conversation follows the model for Active Listening, but Wayne still seems to be resisting unwelcome advice. So his mother tried to move to a deeper level:

MOM: I feel as though there is something else you want me to know.

WAYNE: Yes, there is. I'd be embarrassed to carry around a great big Day Runner. Nobody does that. It's really nerdy.

MOM: I can understand that. You'd look like a nerd being the only kid in school with a big, thick Day Runner.

WAYNE: Sure. And besides, I don't need it. I've been writing my assignments on notebook paper in my binder, and I haven't missed any assignments. Well, I did miss those two English assignments, but that wasn't because I didn't have them written down.

MOM: So you feel you are recording all of your assignments and getting them done, without the expense, inconvenience, and embarrassment of a Day Runner.

WAYNE: That's right. Look, Mom. I think I've been really good about doing my work and turning it in. So when you keep suggesting that I get a Day Runner, it feels as though you think I am being irresponsible and not doing my work. It's like an insult.

At that point, Wayne's mother understood the real message. Wayne had felt insulted, and he hadn't felt safe enough to reveal his real feelings. Her whole attitude and posture changed, and she said, "Wayne, I'm sorry. I didn't know you were writing down all your assignments, and I can see that my nagging about the Day Runner was insulting. I'm sorry for acting without knowing all the facts and for thinking that I know best about everything. I'll have to learn to treat you more like the responsible young adult that you are."

After that breakthrough, Wayne and his mother hugged. They seemed a great deal closer, more cooperative, and more loving than when they started. Wayne felt his mother was accepting his growing up, so he didn't need to be defiant or defensive to establish his independence. His decreased defiance impressed his mother as a sign of maturity, so she felt less need to manage his life. Their relationship was back on a positive path of successes.

You Get a Turn, Too

Active Listening is a tool for when a discussion gets heated. Either you or your teen can notice that you're getting into deep water and say, "Let's be careful to avoid a fight here. Let's use Active Listening. I'll listen to you, then you listen to me." Take turns as many times as needed. When everyone is calm and open, you can drop the formalities and just talk.

As powerful and wonderful as it is, Active Listening is just a technique. You can't use it in all situations, and it won't always work. If your teen asks what's for dinner, don't say, "It seems you are hungry." In routine conversations, and when the channel of communication is open, just talk normally. Save Active Listening to handle the breakdowns.

Chapter 4 Key Points

1. To get your teen to talk and listen, the first step is to get her to talk.

2. To get her to talk, be a good listener. Conversation will start as soon as your teen feels that you will listen attentively and with empathy. It won't start as long as she feels you are likely to ignore or argue with whatever she says.

3. When communication is strained, use Active Listening.

4. Be accepting and empathetic. Hearing the other person's point of view doesn't mean you agree.

5. Keep listening until the channel for communication is open. If needed, dig deeper for the real story. Don't try to send any messages until the channel is open.

6. Use I-messages. Avoid questions that sound like an interrogation or an order, or that imply criticism. Change from "Have you done your homework?" to "I'd like to know where you stand on your homework."

7. When the channel is open, ask your teen to use Active Listening when listening to you.

8. If your teen won't talk at all, respond to her body language. If she just grunts, reflect back the message you get from the grunt. For example, "You seem upset that I want to talk to you about school."

Chapter 5

Making Agreements to Succeed

The Next Step

Active Listening by itself can solve lots of problems, especially those that arise from a teen's feeling unworthy and unlovable. But even with an open channel of communication and full knowledge of what's going on in your teen's life and mind, there are substantive issues to be handled. This chapter describes some ways of having meetings or discussions, and making agreements to handle issues like homework, curfew, room cleaning, and other household chores.

An Outline for Success

Here is an outline of how to proceed in making a plan for improving any situation with your teen. This isn't the only possible model, nor will it apply exactly to every issue. But it does provide a logical sequence to follow.

- Choose an area in which you would like to see progress.
- Arrange a meeting to work on that area. Include all the family members involved in this issue.
- At the meeting, express your intentions and desires.
- Discuss the issue so everyone knows where everyone else stands.
- Agree on a realistic goal for the next week.
- Agree on what each person is to do.
- Agree on the consequences for the various possible outcomes.
- Write down the agreement.
- Get commitments from everyone to do his or her part.
- Review performance at the end of the week.
- Acknowledge anything and everything positive that anyone has done.
- If appropriate, revise the goal and plan for the coming week.

Details on each of these steps are presented in the sections that follow, in this chapter and the next.

Choose a Target

Take time to decide what you want to happen. If you are upset, wait until you are calm. Then choose one area to work on, two at the most. You can't focus on too many things at once. Perhaps look over the questionnaire on pages 154–55 to identify the one or two things that would make the most difference. If you can make progress on these, other things will fall into place. When you are ready to talk with your teen about the issue, call a family meeting.

Family Meetings

In a business, the goals and everyone's responsibilities for reaching those goals are quite well defined. Even so, people who work together find it worthwhile to have regular meetings to review progress, set priorities, and handle upsets. In the same way, people who live together should have weekly family meetings. According to the book *Systematic Training for Effective Parenting of Teens*, by Don Dinkmeyer and Gary D. McKay, family meetings provide each person the opportunity:

- To be heard
- To express positive feelings about other family members
- To give encouragement

- To agree upon fair distribution of chores
- To express concerns, feelings, and complaints
- To help settle conflicts and deal with recurring issues
- To participate in planning family recreation.

Each person in the family should get a chance to express himself or herself. The meeting is not only a time for parents to tell teens how to behave. It is also a time for teens to tell parents how they feel and how they would like to be treated.

Depending on your family's style and preferences, your family meetings may be more or less informal. Here are some guidelines for a fairly formal approach. Use what you like and ignore the rest.

- Establish a specific weekly meeting time.
- Rotate who is chairperson and secretary.
- Establish and stick to time limits.
- Make sure all members have a chance to offer ideas.
- Encourage everyone to bring up issues.
- Don't permit meetings to become gripe sessions.
- Distribute chores fairly.
- Plan family fun.
- Use your communications skills.
- Evaluate the meeting.
- Evaluate decisions at the next meeting.

If an issue can't be delayed until your regular family meeting, arrange a special meeting.

At any point in scheduling or conducting a family meeting, if the channel of communication is not open, use Active Listening.

Declare Your Intentions

In suggesting that the family work on an issue, take time to declare your intentions. Though you may think your intentions are obvious, a full preamble is often helpful.

Look, Johnny. I'm really interested in making some progress on taking out the garbage. I hope we can discuss it and come to a better solution. We agreed that taking out the garbage is your job. But it seems to me you never do it and you leave it for me. I get angry about it almost every day. I feel you don't appreciate the things I do for you. Also I'm uneasy that I'm not doing my job as a parent. I feel I'm supposed to teach you to be responsible, and it looks to me like I'm not succeeding. I want to clear this up.

Notice how using I-messages puts forth a very clear statement of what is going on, who is responsible, and what the parent wants—all without blaming, insulting, or moralizing.

Discuss the Issue

Before trying to reach agreements, get all the cards on the table. Be sure everyone has been heard. Then all of you can begin to make suggestions about what to do.

Don't Split the Difference

The family is obviously not a country, so political processes and analogies don't necessarily apply. Rather than voting or having someone dictate what will happen, work toward mutual agreement.

You are looking for agreements that—all things considered—everyone is willing to live with. "All things considered" means exactly that. Each person's needs, wants, feelings, and real bargaining chips must be considered. Parents own the house, control most of the money, and have certain responsibilities toward and authority over minor children. So they have real powers they can and should exercise in getting teens to do some things. But even with all that power, a parent can't, for example, force a teenager to enjoy school.

Finding the best agreement is like negotiating a good contract. Negotiating doesn't mean getting the better of the other person. The best agreement is a win-win situation. Everyone can come out better because you all have the same goals. You all want your teen to be safe, happy, and growing toward responsible adulthood. So you are going to try to figure out something that will work for everyone. Don't cave in or accept an agreement you can't live with, and don't expect your teen to do that, either.

Sometimes people think of negotiation as a tug-of-war, ending in a compromise about halfway between what each person wanted. But splitting the difference will rarely produce the best result. In a classic Bible story, King Solomon orders a baby cut in half to satisfy the two women claiming the child. While that "split-the-difference" solution was acceptable to the false claimant, the real mother was willing to give up her half to save her child.

Here's a less extreme example of how splitting the difference may not produce the best solution. Suppose your teen wants to return home from a Saturday night rock concert at four A.M., but you want him home at his regular curfew, which is midnight. One "split-the-difference" solution would be to compromise on two A.M. But that isn't the only possibility, and it probably isn't the best solution for either of you.

To find the best solution, you need to identify the key issues. For example, you might be willing to allow your teen to come in at two A.M., but he can't get a ride unless he waits until the end of the concert at four A.M. So you might pick him up or pay for a taxi. Alternatively, you might be inclined to let him stay out until four, but you are mainly concerned about his being well rested for a family brunch the next morning. If that is the key issue, it might be handled by his getting lots of sleep Friday night or taking a nap on Saturday. And of course, there will be times when the best solution is for him to be home by midnight, even if it means missing the concert. Parents can and should say no to some requests. And they can and should grant special requests on occasion.

Realistic, Near-Term Goals

For any issue, try to define a small change that can realistically be done in the next week. A two-week goal may be necessary in some cases, but a month is probably too long and a semester definitely is. Choose a weekly goal that is almost certain to be achieved. Because it is critical to start a pattern of successes, it is more important to successfully reach 100 percent of a small step forward than to achieve part of a more ambitious goal.

No Halfhearted Agreements

Suppose your teen says, "Trust me. I'll do my homework and get better grades. No problem. I was fooling around before, but now I'm really going to do it." Some of you have heard that before. If you don't believe it, don't accept it, and say so.

Keep talking until *you* feel your teen has made a real commitment to keeping the agreement. Sometimes teens offer you compensation to convince you they mean business: "If I don't get a B average for the quarter, you can ground me for the rest of the semester." If you were dealing with a contractor remodeling your home, a penalty clause is probably necessary. But you really want the job done well and on time, not the penalties. So don't use a strong penalty clause as a substitute for serious commitment.

Consequences, Rewards, and Punishments

Nearly all books about parenting discuss natural and logical consequences, and there is general agreement among most authors. Still, most of the books are written for parents of children younger than thirteen, so based on my experience with high-school students and their parents, here are my views and suggestions.

First of all, the natural consequences of a teen's behavior are *natural*—that is, you don't have to do anything to set them up or carry them out. The natural consequence of staying up late is being tired, of doing your homework is learning, and so on.

However, many natural consequences are too distant or too dangerous for a child to understand: a child may not yet appreciate the long-term benefits of learning algebra, and we certainly don't want him to experience the natural consequences of reckless driving. Where the natural consequences are too dangerous, or are too remote or too slight to motivate a teen, some psychologists suggest adding logical consequences—rewards or punishments. In doing that, it is easy to go wrong.

The natural consequences for doing homework include learning, feeling smart, feeling school is easier and more fun, getting good grades, and finding more college and job opportunities. But despite those substantial rewards, many teens are unmotivated for school. They seem to be too childish to understand and appreciate those rewards. It seems those rewards are inadequate to get them to do homework rather than talk on the phone or watch TV. So since the natural consequences seem inadequate, many parents attempt to motivate their teens through rewards and punishments. Unfortunately, this rarely succeeds, so let me recommend a different approach.

To start with, remember that your teen values education and wants to succeed. If he isn't doing the work, the problem is more than likely to be one or more of the three barriers to success in school. Those barriers are not addressed by the usual rewards and punishments— things like money, cars, clothes, vacations, telephones, late curfews, or the withholding of those rewards. And if the real problem is not being addressed, it is likely to get worse rather than go away. So using ordinary rewards and punishments—like money and grounding—usually won't work.

The most desired rewards in life are feelings of security, love, and success. We get those feelings from our actual accomplishments and from expressions of respect and esteem, especially from our families and ourselves. So in making agreements, do not minimize the intangible payoffs of being acknowledged for having done what was agreed and having met the goal. If your teen goes from a C to a B in a course, his own sense of accomplishment and your being pleased may be more motivating, more rewarding, than the benefits attached to higher school grades. If you devalue that reward by immediately focusing on his going from B to A, your teen may decide there's no pleasing you.

In addition to the very important, intangible rewards of approval and acceptance, and in addition to the natural consequences of accomplishment, material rewards can be an added incentive. Like a birthday present, an extra reward is a token of appreciation, not payment in full. So such extra rewards are not necessary or recommended. Presents are different. It is fine to give an unexpected present as a tangible expression of your delight at some accomplishment, or just to say "I love you." So from time to time, when you are thinking nice thoughts about your teen, buy him a little gift.

Punishment

Now let's talk about punishment. A punishment, obviously, is something that causes pain. The idea, of course, is to convince your teen to do the right thing or not do the wrong thing. Some obvious examples of punishments are spanking or hitting, grounding your teen, sending him to his room, or reducing his allowance. Punishments make teens resentful and frequently produce results counter to what you intend. So I definitely recommend that you *do not punish* your teen. Whatever the pros and cons may be for younger children, punishment is too likely to backfire with teens. This does not mean that you can't make demands on your teen. Nor does it mean that you permit him to do whatever he likes. It simply means that you don't do anything with the primary intention of causing physical or mental pain or exacting some penalty from your teen.

For some parents, punishment seems a natural and perhaps essential way of controlling and guiding children. If that is true for you, my advice that you stop using punishment would be a major change. I ask that you read this entire chapter and then think about whether punishment is a necessary and useful part of your relationship with your teen.

Sometimes we get into situations in which the loss of a reward feels like a punishment. For example, suppose some parents, intending to provide an incentive, tell their teen they'll buy him a car if he gets a 3.5 average (B-plus) for the year. Assuming that he put forth a reasonable effort, if the teen doesn't earn the reward, he will be deeply disappointed. He may be so discouraged that his motivation goes down.

Whether you call this outcome a punishment may be a matter of semantics. But the important point is this: Negative outcomes are potentially defeating. So be extremely cautious not only about punishment, but also about offering big rewards in situations in which the chance of success is low. Positive outcomes are much more likely to produce further achievement. So always try to make agreements that are likely to succeed.

Here's an example of an agreement that is likely to cause problems. Allen and his parents agreed that if he did not get a B average at midterm, he would be grounded for the rest of the semester. If Allen fails, he gets punished in a major way. Even though his parents hope being grounded will ensure that Allen has enough time at home to study, he is basically under house arrest. He will definitely experience this as punishment rather than time management. Avoid agreements like this.

In contrast to this last example, Ben and his parents agreed that he would finish any homework left from the week on Saturday before he went out for the evening. This is not punishment. This is an agreement to arrange work and play in a logical sequence and to complete the work before playing. This agreement is very likely to help Ben get his work done and to learn to manage time.

Here's another example of what not to do. Amy and her parents agreed she could use the family car on weekends if she maintained a B average. When her grades fell, her parents followed through and denied her the use of the car. Amy still went out, getting rides from her friends. She was only mildly inconvenienced, but she was very annoyed. Though she had understood and accepted the arrangement, the outcome now seemed unreasonable. Though she tried to work harder, she actually did less schoolwork and her grades declined further.

If B grades would result in a significant reduction in

the cost of car insurance, there is a real, and therefore more acceptable, reason to link grades and use of the car. But if there isn't such a strong external reason to link Amy's use of the car to her school performance, it would be better to deal with school separately from the use of the car.

Here's a pair of good examples about curfew. Dan stayed out past his agreed-to curfew at midnight, so his parents changed his curfew to eleven P.M. for the next two weekends. Though this was clearly a punishment, it was at least mild, short-term, and directly related to the behavior being punished. That's about as good as you can do with punishment.

When Bob stayed out past his agreed-to curfew, his father said, "Your being out late makes it difficult for me to rely on you. Also, your coming in late woke me up, which I think is unfair. I'd like to arrange things so that won't happen again." In response, Bob said he was sorry both for waking his parents and for breaking the agreement. Bob said, "It won't happen again." His father felt Bob's commitment was sincere and answered, "Okay. I accept your commitment. This incident is closed."

Penalty Clauses

Parents often hesitate to make agreements that seemingly have no penalties. Curfew violations provide a good example. Suppose you and your teen agree to a precise twelve o'clock curfew. Then he comes home at twelve-thirty A.M. without a good "the car wouldn't start" excuse. Don't you have to do something? No, you really don't have to exact some price. Your teen is practicing to mastery and still needs more practice. Probably it would be enough to talk about it at the next family meeting:

> You were out past your agreed-upon curfew on Saturday night. I was disappointed about that, and at the time I was both worried and angry. You seemed sincere when you said you were sorry, but I don't want apologies. We should both be able to rely on your doing what you say you'll do, especially in situations like going out on Saturday night. Leaving a party or a concert at a time you've committed to is part of learning how to look out for yourself.

With curfews and other issues, a sincere commitment from the teen should be accepted. Remember, the idea is for him to be safe and to learn to manage himself. If your teen isn't yet skillful enough to see to his own safety on Saturday nights, then as a responsible parent you have to do it for him. That may mean changing the curfew to eleven P.M. or taking control over how the rides are being handled. Though he's not going to like those arrangements, that's not punishment; that's taking care of him until he is ready to do it for himself. Using punishment is appealing as a way to "teach someone a lesson." But the added incentive is artificial and doesn't contribute to his practicing and learning to manage himself and keep his commitments.

Again, let me repeat, punishment usually doesn't work in a family. Society punishes criminals and penalizes illegal left turns. But that's different. You are trying to help your teen learn to be responsible for himself. If he hasn't mastered something, he needs more practice, and probably some more encouragement. Punishment, rather than increasing motivation, is likely to generate hostility or discouragement. Find out as best you can what went wrong, and then figure out how to get him moving up his own learning curve again. If he hasn't yet mastered keeping himself safe, delegate less control to him and manage the situation yourself for a while longer. With this view, you will be less tempted to use punishment to change your teen's behavior.

Broken Agreements

If an agreement is broken, don't immediately decide to increase the rewards or punishments. Agreements are rarely broken because the reward or punishment was too small. Remember that everyone wants to succeed and nothing succeeds like success. So if an agreement is not kept, find out what went wrong before trying to decide on the solution. Maybe everyone's expectations were too high. To go from no homework to 100 percent in one week may be too much to expect. Consider making the next week's goal easier. Maybe the agreement didn't cover some important issue that came up by surprise. Or perhaps a parent broke the agreement. For example, suppose the father agreed not to nag for a week but lost control when he saw his son watching TV the night before a test. The father broke the agreement, and in retaliation—consciously or unconsciously—his son didn't do his homework for the rest of the week. Should we punish the son for causing his father to break the agreement? Should we punish the father? Probably neither action will help. After getting clear about what happened without blaming anyone, the family should decide what they intend to do in the next week.

Jeanine promised her parents she would work hard and get at least a B-minus in math. When she got a C-minus for a midterm grade, her parents decided to ground her until her grades improved. Their intention was to ensure that Jeanine would spend more time studying, but Jeanine considered this too harsh a punishment. In retaliation, she stopped studying math entirely and ended the semester with a D. As a result Jeanine was grounded for the rest of the school year. Her parents felt obligated to stick to their word, and she grew more and more resentful. As you might expect, all her grades went down that year. Even more unfortunately, she and her parents couldn't get along. They spoke less and less, and usually with annoyance and anger. Jeanine eventually graduated and spent three years halfheartedly going to a community college. Then she gave up on school completely.

When the same situation arose for Marla, she and her parents were able to discuss the situation fully. They were able to see that Marla had been doing her work fairly regularly. With that recognition, Marla was willing to commit to doing more to get the better results that she and they wanted. Together they agreed that until her math scores improved, Marla would spend two hours each Saturday working on any missed assignments and reviewing. She agreed to put in those two hours before going out on Saturday night.

The next Saturday, Marla spent two hours at her desk, minus the time for two phone calls and two trips to the kitchen for snacks. What would you have said? Her parents thought about it and decided that the cup was half full, rather than half empty. They told Marla they were really impressed that she had kept her agreement to spend extra time trying to master a subject that she feared. As you might expect, Marla's math grades got better.

Sample Agreements

To help you understand the ideas in this chapter, following are sample agreements about chores, room cleaning, and curfew, and a series of agreements about homework. These are intended as examples to guide you and your teen in making agreements that apply to his situation. You may want to proceed in smaller or larger steps toward the ultimate goal, and your first step may be higher or lower than in these examples.

Chores

Mike is to take out the garbage every night before going to bed. Since his mom and dad are unwilling to have the garbage stay in the kitchen if he forgets, the family reached this agreement:

> Anytime Mike goes to bed without taking out the garbage, Mom or Dad will do it, and whoever does will receive $1 from Mike for the assistance with his chore. We will review this arrangement each week. (This isn't punishment. The $1 payment is a fair payment for assistance.)

Room Cleaning

Here is a sample agreement that clarifies exactly what is expected:

> Troy is to clean his room *every day*. This means no clothes lying around, laundry goes in the hamper, food and dishes get returned to the kitchen, and personal things should be neatly arranged. If company is coming, and on Saturdays and Sundays, he is to make his bed. Troy is not to leave the house on Friday night, Saturday, or Sunday until Mom or Dad agrees that his room is clean. At the end of the week we will review the situation.

There is no penalty clause in this agreement, which is perfectly satisfactory. Also, this agreement doesn't prohibit reminding or nagging. If nagging is a problem, the agreement should be amended accordingly.

Curfew

The ultimate goal is for Bill to be able to manage his time and social life so he can enjoy his leisure time and be reasonably safe. Toward that goal, depending on his age and maturity, he and his parents might have an agreement like this:

Bill is to be home no later than ten P.M. on weeknights and midnight on Fridays and Saturdays. These times are exact, with no grace period. Whenever he goes out, Bill is to tell Mom and Dad where he will be, who is driving, what he will be doing, with whom, and approximately when he will return. If the situation changes in any important way, he is to call and get approval to go elsewhere or do anything else. Mom and Dad may veto Bill's going to unchaperoned parties, using or being around others using drugs or alcohol, or driving with anyone they don't trust as a driver. If Mom or Dad is unavailable to approve any outing, but if all aspects of the outing are things they have previously approved, Bill may leave a note and go; otherwise he may not.

An agreement like this should be modified and re-laxed as Bill demonstrates responsibility and skill in looking after his own well-being. Also notice this agreement only addresses the time, place, and activity of Bill's going out. It doesn't cover Bill having to do his homework or chores before going out. If those are important issues, the agreement should cover who decides and on what basis.

Homework

The ultimate goal is for Kyle to take complete responsibility for his homework, doing it regularly, and mastering his courses. Getting to that goal from where Kyle is today in terms of performance and responsibility may take a few weeks to several months. Working toward that goal, the family might enter into a series of agreements like these.

1. For the next week, Kyle will write down 100 percent of his assignments, including due dates. If he is absent from a class, by the end of his first day back he will get the assignments from a teacher or a reliable classmate.

Kyle will do homework from seven to nine-thirty P.M. Sunday through Thursday. During that time he will not watch TV or talk on the phone. Mom and Dad will not remind him or nag him. They will make their own observations about what

Kyle is doing. He may have a friend over to work on particular assignments, but only with the prior approval of Mom or Dad. If something comes up that interferes with his working during those hours, Kyle will make up the lost time on Friday afternoon, and, if necessary, also on Sunday.

Also, he will note the date he completes each assignment and the date he turns it in. He will show Mom or Dad his assignment list every night around nine P.M. Mom and Dad will not nag. They will merely notice what he has or hasn't done. At the end of this week, we will review Kyle's performance and make plans for next week.

If, based on past problems, Kyle's mom and dad cannot rely on him to tell the truth about whether he has gone to school, whether there are assignments, and whether he has turned them in, then there is a double problem. The major problem is the lack of honesty in the relationship. The lesser, but still important problem is his school performance. Both can and should be addressed simultaneously.

Some parents might feel that Kyle needs to be coaxed and coerced into telling the truth with threats and punishments. But consider why Kyle is unable or unwilling to tell them the truth. It is probably not that he prefers lying in an absolute sense. Almost everyone I've met preferred the feelings of integrity and closeness generated by honesty and openness. Rather, Kyle is probably driven by some embarrassment or fear. The problem may be very trivial, involving just a minor reaction to peer pressure, a teacher, or his parents. Or the problem may be a quite deep and complex personality or character issue, requiring the assistance of a therapist. Unless and until they decide professional help is needed, his parents should try to help Kyle feel safe enough to first confide in them, and then change his behavior.

At the same time, his parents should probably arrange with the school to provide weekly reports from all Kyle's teachers. Being a normal teenager, Kyle will fight this like the devil. He'll say he is offended by their lack of trust, by being accused of being a liar. But his mom and dad may need to hold firm on this. Though this will be embarrassing and onerous, it is temporary. They have the responsibility to know what's going on and also to assist him in learning to build a reputation for honesty and responsibility with them, with the world, and with himself. As he demonstrates responsibility, they will be able to rely on getting accurate information from him and can drop the reports from teachers.

2. For the second week, Kyle is to record all of his assignments and complete and turn in at least 80 percent of them on time. He is to study from seven to nine-thirty, or make up the time on the weekend. Each night they are home, Mom or Dad will inspect Kyle's homework at about nine or nine-thirty P.M. They will notice and comment on how well done it is, and may ask questions to determine

whether Kyle has mastered the material. They will not nag or order Kyle to do more.

3. The third week Kyle is to complete at least 90 percent of his assignments on time, while managing his own time. Kyle may do his homework on whatever schedule he chooses, but Mom or Dad will inspect his homework every night.

4. In the fourth week Kyle is to completely manage his own homework. Mom and Dad will review each week's results based on Kyle's records of assignments completed and turned in.

Chapter 5 Key Points

1. Work on no more than one or two issues at a time.
2. State your intentions fully and carefully.
3. At a family meeting or a special meeting, discuss the issue. Use Active Listening to open the channel of communication and keep it open.
4. Devise a realistic, practical agreement that is a step in the right direction. It is important to successfully reach the goal, even if it is just a small step forward. Achieving 100 percent of a smaller goal is more beneficial. This should be a win-win agreement that, all things considered, everyone can live with. Don't vote, don't split the difference just to be agreeable, don't cave in, don't expect anyone else to do so, either.
5. Don't accept halfhearted commitments.
6. Set up a definite time period—usually one week—for reviewing progress and making changes in the agreement as needed.
7. Good agreements don't need rewards and punishments. Sometimes rewards are okay. Punishment doesn't work.
8. If an agreement fails, don't immediately decide to punish. Consider the overall goal of having your teen learn by practicing. Then find a new

agreement that is likely to start a series of successes. You may have to take back some control to assure your teen's safety while he is practicing to mastery in this area.

Chapter 6

Encouragement

When Jill got her first A on an English composition, she was anxious to tell everyone in the family. The first to hear the news was her younger brother. He said, "Awesome. Is there any ice cream in the fridge?"

When her mom heard, she said, "That's great, Jill. I always knew you could do it. And you see, Mrs. Proll doesn't dislike you."

Dad said, "Jill, that was a great paper and with a little more work I'm sure you are going to do much better than you ever thought you could."

Then Jill got on the phone and told her friend Beth about the A paper. Beth said, "Wow, Jill, that's great. It must feel wonderful." Jill went on to tell Beth that she was indeed very proud and pleased. Jill explained how she hadn't known how to get started, but had been watching TV and it just hit her to write about the differences between fiction and real life. Beth said, "Hey, that's pretty deep. But even with that great topic, it must have been a lot of work." In response to Beth's approval and interest, Jill spent ten minutes telling Beth all about how she wrote that paper, including spending a whole hour coming up with a great title. At the end of the phone conversation Jill felt terrific, appreciated, and happy.

Jill was encouraged by Beth. She wasn't by the responses she got from her family. But her parents could have done just what Beth did. They could have responded with sincere approval and interest, taking the occasion to celebrate Jill's success, rather than depreciate it with advice on how to do better.

Love Is the Foundation

As we've said, though you love your teen, she may have self-doubts about being lovable and worthy of your respect and admiration. Younger children's well-being is almost totally based on their parents caring for them. Well-adjusted adults have their own self-esteem at the foundation of their well-being. Teens are in transition. On any given day they may suddenly need reassurance that your love and protection are still there. At other times they are vigorously trying to prove to you and to themselves that they can handle everything on their own. These mood swings are almost as surprising to teens as they are to the parents.

Because of that intermittent need to be reassured of

your love, teens are very sensitive to advice, criticism, requests, and demands from parents. They take offense when none was intended. And they frequently test you in annoying, unskillful, or rebellious ways. All of this makes it difficult for your teen to listen and respond positively when you correct her or request changes in her behavior. This chapter describes some ideas you can use when encouraging your teen to do the things that she ought to do for her own good and for peaceful co-operation within the family.

Notice the Positives

You can best encourage your teen by noticing anything and everything that you consider positive and that makes you feel good about her. Often parents tend to concentrate on how far their teens have to go, rather than acknowledging how far they have come. Without realizing it, they are being too demanding. No matter how your teen is doing, recognize that she is moving along her own learning curve. Learning to be a responsible, independent adult is tougher and takes longer than learning to walk. But your teen needs the same sort of support and approval you gave her then. When your toddler took even one step, you were genuinely delighted, you gushed with praise, snapped her picture, and called the grandparents with the news. You didn't say, "That wobbly step is a good start. But look, you need to cut out falling down and start linking your steps together. There's no reason you can't be running by the end of the semester."

If something pleases you, express it: "I'm pleased you brought your grade up in math." If your teen has brought her grade up in math but you aren't pleased, examine yourself.

All of us can tell when we are being patronized or manipulated, and all of us hate being treated that way. When you are giving a compliment, keep at it until the person feels complimented. Even when you are sincere about a compliment, your teen may feel you don't mean it, that you are just trying to manipulate her to do better. So don't start talking about other things, especially not about further improvements, until you are sure the compliment has been received.

There is a confusing paradox about encouragement. I've just said that to encourage your teen—to help her do the best she can—notice the positives. But if your teen senses that you are doing that to get her to become more worthy, she may resent the implication that she is not worthy now. This paradox is real. Handling it may seem tricky, but it can be done.

The solution is to be clear about your own thoughts and then to take the time and effort to communicate those thoughts to your teen. For example, suppose your teen has raised her French grade from C to B, which is terrific. Now you want to acknowledge that in a way that will encourage her to get an A. But if you do, aren't you really saying B isn't good enough? Not necessarily. Your full view on the situation might be something like this:

- I love you no matter what grades you get.
- Knowing French and getting better grades will be good for you.
- I'm proud of your improvement from C to B, and you should be proud, too.
- I think you can get an A, and I think it would be worth it to you to do the extra or different things needed to get that A.

Communicating all of that to your teen is possible and worthwhile. But it will definitely take at least a few minutes of talking, and maybe not all of it can be handled in one conversation. Having gotten clear about your own thinking, you are much more likely to be able to let her know how you feel. You then won't nullify a compliment unintentionally. You won't make the mistake of saying, "Nice going on raising your French grade to a B, but I think you can do even better and get an A."

Catch Her Doing Something Right

If your teen isn't handling school and life around the house too well, you may think there's nothing you can honestly compliment her on. If that's your situation, you can bet your teen feels she can't do anything well enough to please you or herself. To get out of that bind, hunt for something she does that you think well of. Catch her doing something right, and comment on it. For example, "I've always been impressed with the way you can make and keep friends" or "I admire that you are able to handle being alone when you have to."

Save the Negatives for Sunday

Regardless of how exemplary our teens are, most of us parents would like to help them with just a few more comments and corrections. We feel an urge to tell them how to take the next steps up their learning curves. If they haven't been doing too well at school or have been difficult at home, our list of complaints lengthens and our emotions intensify. This can lead to a lot of nagging, arguing, and threatening, or at least to that impression. To avoid that, when you think of something negative you want to tell your teen, make yourself a note to bring it up at the next family meeting. Before the meeting, look over your notes and decide which things to handle now, and which to leave for later or forget.

Don't Kid Your Kid

Be extremely careful about teasing or making a joke out of something you or your teen takes seriously. If someone is the butt of the joke, that person rarely laughs. When your real intent is to correct or control, don't tease or kid your child. Even when you are in good spirits and are really just kidding, your teen may feel insulted or threatened. If she doesn't laugh, she didn't think it was funny. Say you're sorry for making a bad joke, and talk straight.

Focus on Learning Rather Than on Grades

Good grades indicate successful learning—that the student had the skills and diligence to handle schoolwork successfully. And good grades have real value for such things as college admissions, getting a job, and discounts on auto insurance. But there are some side effects from grades that can have a negative impact on students.

The problem with grades is that, by third, fourth, or fifth grade, students have come to think of themselves as A or B or C or D students. In other words, they have internalized the judgment about themselves represented by their grades. So a C student thinks she is a C student and not an A student. She believes that even if she got A's, by working extremely hard and getting tutoring, it would just be a false front. Despite the A's, she is a C student. Better grades might get her into a more competitive college or career, but it would be a mistake for her. It would put her into competition with real A students and therefore at a disadvantage. So she adjusts her goals and expectations to match what she sees as her limitations. She may also be protecting herself from the embarrassment and disappointment of feeling less competent than she and her parents had hoped.

Parents and teachers try to talk students out of those

self-defeating views of themselves. But the teens don't buy it; the words don't match the students' reality. That's why so many teens seem to lack motivation. The way out of this situation is to focus on her mastering daily assignments, rather than on quarter or semester grades. Mastery learning provides an immediate sense of competence and progress. And, of course, if she learns the material, better grades will follow.

Chapter 6 Key Points

1. The main ingredient in helping your teen build a pattern of success is to encourage her.
2. Things that are encouraging are:
   - *Empathy*. Accepting her as she is.
   - *Attention*. Noticing her and her efforts and progress.
   - *Approval*. Taking pride and pleasure in her and her progress, and communicating that by word and deed.
   - *Trust*. Allowing her to make her own decisions whenever you reasonably can.
3. Things that are discouraging are:
   - *Complaints, nagging, threats, and punishment*. Focusing on shortfalls, shortcomings, failures, lack of mastery.
   - *Ridicule and sarcasm.*
   - *Prodding*. Always mentioning the next step, especially at the moment when the last step was just completed successfully.

Chapter 7

Tutoring Tips

Some Practical Tips for Parents and Students

There are two situations in which tutoring makes a lot of sense: when your teen is trying to catch up on prerequisites, and when your teen needs more, different, or better instruction than he is getting in class.

Tutoring can be very effective. In some studies, 90 percent of tutored students did as well as the top 10 percent of classroom-taught students. But lots of students don't want to be tutored; they won't ask for help from their parents or their teachers, and they resist working with paid tutors. Even among teens who agree to be tutored, tutoring doesn't always work well. This chapter presents some ideas to help increase the benefit your teen gets from tutoring, either by you or by a hired tutor.

Why Teens Don't Ask for Help

Students don't ask for help for some combination of reasons like these:

- Students often feel they'll never be able to master the subject, so tutoring will be a waste of their time and of your time or money.
- They're worried that if they don't improve, despite the added effort and expense of tutoring, then you will be upset with them.
- They are embarrassed to have anyone find out that they don't know their lessons.
- They're afraid the tutor may scold about what hasn't been done in the past, and maybe assign extra work for the future.

If your teen doesn't want a tutor but you think he needs one, try to get to the heart of the matter. The discussion may bring up and resolve significant issues far beyond the question of tutoring.

If your teen is to work with a tutor—either a professional or a peer tutor, or with you—help your teen take charge of the tutoring in the ways I will describe. To be effective, a tutor has to be seen by the student as an ally—someone who is helping him with his problems rather than adding to them.

What Not to Do

Before describing some hints on how to tutor, here's a sample of some of the wrong things for a tutor to do and say.

▪ Scene 1

TEEN: I'm still having trouble with percentages.
TUTOR: I'm not surprised; you haven't been studying much.

▪ Scene 2

TEEN: I hate math and Miss Dewey.
TUTOR: No point in blaming math and Miss Dewey. You can do it, but you're not applying yourself.

▪ Scene 3

TEEN: I'm just no good at math.
TUTOR: You've got to put forth some effort. You are still trying to slide by.

In each of these scenes, the tutor is ignoring or compounding the student's problems. Unless something unexpectedly good starts happening, this student is going to try to avoid further sessions with this tutor.

Suggestions for Tutoring

Here are five suggestions for effective tutoring:

The Student Is in Charge

During a tutoring session, the student is the client. If you are tutoring your own teen, it may seem strange to think of him as your client. After all, as the parent, you are in charge. But if you want to be an effective tutor, you have to serve the client, even if he is your child and even if he isn't paying for your services.

Similarly, if you are considering hiring a tutor for your teen, ask the tutor about his style. And after you hire a tutor, when you observe him with your teen, or when you talk to the tutor or your teen, consider this issue. Your teen will benefit most from tutoring that addresses his concerns. If the tutor is too controlling, your teen may feel that the tutoring is like adding another course to his work load.

So any tutor—whether it is you or a hired tutor— should let the student determine:

- What he wants to work on
- When he wants a demonstration or explanation of how to do something

- When he wants a question answered or an answer repeated or rephrased
- When he wants another problem of the same difficulty, a harder one, or an easier one
- When he wants to keep thinking or working on a problem.
- When he wants feedback
- How and when he wants to be quizzed or tested

Sometimes the student doesn't know what he should work on next. So he should say to the tutor: "I really don't know how to attack this. Where's a good place to begin?"

Sometimes the tutor thinks the student is making a poor decision, such as giving up too quickly on a problem and asking for the answer. The tutor might say something like this: "I'll tell you the answer if you want me to. But I think you ought to try a little longer to figure it out for yourself." But the decision is up to the student.

When there are safety problems, as in learning to drive or fly an airplane, the tutor may have to take control to avoid accidents. But otherwise, the idea is for the student to be actively in charge, with the tutor in a responsive, reactive mode.

Show Me, Let Me Try, Tell Me How I'm Doing

The basic sequence in learning, with or without a tutor, is this:

1. *Show me.* The tutor (or teacher or book or film) explains and/or demonstrates what the student is to do.
2. *Let me try.* The learner begins to practice.
3. *Tell me how I'm doing.* The teacher or tutor provides feedback, correcting inappropriate practice but especially noting the things being done correctly or better. Practice should continue until the tutor and the student both agree the student has mastered the material.

With this model, the tutor doesn't have to be a master teacher. He just has to be able to demonstrate doing the work, explain how he did it, and check the student's work. So if you know a subject, you can tutor even though you might not feel prepared to give lectures and teach the course. This also explains why students do so well as tutors of other students.

Be Patient

When anyone talks about a tutor he likes, he will almost always mention that the tutor is "so patient." A good tutor gives the student the feeling that the student's rate of learning is acceptable. Just as there is no point in trying to tell someone something until the channel of communication is open, tutoring should move at the student's pace. Using the mastery learning idea, don't move ahead until the student has mastered the current point and is ready for the next. In a classroom situation, the teacher may not know whether everyone has understood a particular point, and even if he did, it might not be practical to allow for those who need further information or time. But the essence of tutoring is to pace the teaching and practice to the student's learning rate.

Most tutors have the intention to be patient. But most of us who have done any tutoring know that we tutors frequently feel impatient, and we often show that to our students. If you are tutoring, here are some hints to help you be patient. If you are observing a tutor you have hired for your teen, you can compare the tutor's behavior to these hints.

First of all, remember the student will learn by practicing. So though a tutor may tell or show a student how to do something, the student has to practice. While the student practices, the tutor has little or nothing to do. The tutor might watch the student start on some practice to make sure he is using the right approach. But then the student will continue practicing, leaving the tutor nothing to do until the student needs some help or has mastered that material and is ready for something new.

As a rough guide, more than half the time, the tutor has nothing to do. That is why many tutoring services put two or three or more students with one tutor. At first you might think one-on-one tutoring would be better, though more costly, than small-group tutoring. But generally tutoring is more effective with several students, and the students like it better. So if you are tutoring your teen, plan to have time on your hands during the tutoring. Arm yourself with something to make the waiting easier. You might read the newspaper or something else you won't mind interrupting each time your student asks for help. Don't watch TV, even with headphones, because the picture will distract your teen.

If you are paying a tutor by the hour, there is a tendency to expect the tutor to be earning his fee by teaching throughout the session. But the tutor should do nothing—except maybe read the newspaper—while waiting for your teen to finish practicing. So don't judge a tutor by the amount of lecturing and demonstrating he does.

When you are tutoring, you may also lose patience over the way in which your teen is handling his time, his schoolwork, or other things. If you want the tutoring to work, try to resist all parental urges to lecture, scold, admonish, criticize, advise, and counsel. Save all of that for a time when you are in your parent role, such as the weekly family meeting. In tutoring, the student is the client and, within the bounds of normal courtesy, is entitled to give orders to the tutor—whether the tutor is you or anyone else.

For example, if your student asks for the spelling of a word and you know it, tell him. Don't take that as an opportunity to make him use a dictionary. But when you are not tutoring, if your teen calls to you to spell words, you can reasonably say no. Be sure to discuss the differences between the two situations so you are both clear about it.

How to Help When You Don't Know the Subject

If you don't know the subject, you can't demonstrate and provide feedback. But you can still help in several ways. Most important, you can help your student learn to manage his homework. Initially, you may want to check daily that he knows what is required and has the supplies he needs. See if he is clear about how to prepare to practice and what type of practice to do. You may also want to spend a few minutes each day reviewing how he is going to manage his homework time that day. Finally, at the end of the evening, you may want to go over the homework and how he did it.

As an example, Brian's parents were always at work when he got home from school each day. So they agreed that each day Brian would plan his work and call his dad at about four P.M. If he was unable to take the call, his dad would call back as soon as he could. On a typical day, Brian might say, "I've got three assignments for tonight: French, math, and some reading for English. I think it will take me about half an hour for each. I'm going to do the French right now. Then I'm going out until dinner. After dinner, I'll do the math at seven-thirty, then I'll do the reading. So I ought to be done about eight-thirty, maybe nine at the latest, even if I get a couple of phone calls."

What you do and how often you do it should be defined and agreed to in advance for each week. As your teen gets into good habits about writing down assignments, planning his time, and completing his work to mastery, you will reduce what you do and how often you do it.

In addition to dealing with the managing of homework and time, you may be able to offer useful advice about how to practice. Even without knowing the subject, you may be able to assist your teen in choosing the best way to practice based simply on your greater experience. You might be guided by the suggestions in Chapter 2. You will recall that the key idea is practicing whatever is supposed to be learned. In school, that generally means the practice should be very similar to the test.

If your teen needs help in a subject you don't know, you might be willing to learn along with your teen. For a typical course, this might take you five to ten hours per week, which is a fairly major commitment. But if you are willing to put in the time, you should try this. Parents who do almost always say that it worked well and was enjoyable. They are also pleasantly surprised at how quickly and easily they are able to learn subjects they no longer remember or that once gave them trouble.

Practice to Mastery

Listening, watching, and reading will not produce mastery of the tasks students have to perform on tests. So even with a tutor, the student still has to practice to mastery. You may have been surprised by the example in which the student told the tutor to spell a word. If the student is in charge, doesn't that allow the student to direct the tutor to do all the work? If the student is working for mastery, the answer is no. Since the student is going for mastery, no matter how many problems the tutor does, the assignment isn't complete until the student has practiced to mastery.

Now suppose your teen has finished his homework. You might look it over or ask him about it. Try to find out whether he has mastered the material and whether he knows that he has mastered it. If he has mastered any of it, be sure to comment on that. Whether you should suggest or order him to continue to mastery depends on the agreement you have about homework at that time.

Your conversation might sound like this:

MOM: Mark, how did you do with that math assignment?

MARK: I finished it.

MOM: You don't sound too happy about it.

MARK: Well, it was pretty hard.

MOM: Let me see. Your work looks very neat. I suppose you checked the answers in the back of the book.

MARK: Sure, for the odd-numbered problems. There are no answers for the even ones.

MOM: I can't check your work, but do you understand it? Have you mastered, um, what is this, factoring?

MARK: Yeah. It is completing the square, and I mostly understand it. But I really don't know how to do problems like these.

MOM: What is your plan about that?

MARK: Well, this is the newest material, so I think she will explain it again tomorrow. If I'm still stuck, I'll get together with Jimmy on Saturday. He'll be able to show me how to do it.

MOM: Hey, that sounds very responsible. I'm impressed.

MARK: Thanks.

MOM: Let me remind you that you were planning to go to the beach with Cy this Saturday.

MARK: Oh, that's right. Well, I'll handle that with Jimmy either Friday or Sunday.

Getting Started

If you and your teen decide you or a tutor will be helping him with homework, tell your teen about what you've read in this chapter or have him read it himself. Then discuss and agree to the ground rules for any tutoring you will do. These may be the guidelines we've presented, or some modifications of your own. Make notes about your agreements, including when you will be available and how he can make an appointment with you. For example, your ground rules might be something like this:

- Mom available every Thursday evening from seven to eight, to help with math.
- Darren in charge of what is covered, how many problems, etc.

- During the tutoring session, Mom won't nag about homework, math, trying harder, cleaning up room, etc.
- Darren may end the session whenever he likes.

Until things are going very smoothly, take a moment to review your ground rules together at the start of each tutoring session. After the session, review how each of you felt about your interaction.

As with anything else, practice makes perfect. With a little practice you can be a valuable resource for your teen, and you'll probably feel terrific that he wants and values your assistance. If you get into conflict during the tutoring, call a time-out. Use Active Listening to find out what is going wrong.

Hiring a Tutor

If and when you and your teen agree to hire a tutor, consider letting your teen contact and interview the tutor. This is a tall order, but if he can do it, let him. It will build his skills and start the tutor-client relationship on the right basis—namely, with the learner in charge. There is little chance that your teen will choose the wrong tutor—for example, a tutor who doesn't know the subject adequately.

There are professional tutors, but you should definitely consider peer tutors as well. Many high schools have successful peer-tutoring programs. Peer tutors are often very effective and well liked by their students. They charge less and are conveniently available during study periods at school, as well as after school.

If your teen doesn't value the tutor's help, something is wrong. The issue may be just about the tutor, or it may be something more general about school or life. In any event, find out what the issue is and clear it up. If the issue is just your teen's reaction to the particular tutor, and if discussions with the tutor don't resolve the problem, get another tutor.

Chapter 7 Key Points

1. Tutoring can be very helpful. Talk over the situation with your teen. Get agreement before taking action. Consider using another student as a peer tutor.

2. The student is in charge. If you are doing the tutoring, your role is that of helper rather than parent or teacher.

3. A good model for learning with a tutor is: Show me. Let me try. Tell me how I'm doing. In other words, preparation, practice, and feedback.

4. The tutor must be patient and have some activity—like reading the paper—to pass the time while the student is practicing.

5. Even if you don't know the subject, you may be able to tutor your teen in how to manage doing his homework. If and when you do that, you are a tutor and the tutoring rules apply.

6. Practice is essential. If the tutor fills the session with teaching, the student will have to practice later, on his own. An effective tutor may be waiting while the student practices during half of each session with a student.

7. If your teen doesn't value his time with a tutor, ask the tutor to do things differently. If that doesn't work, get a new tutor.

Chapter 8

Books and Supplies

A Place for Everything

Your teen needs a relatively peaceful place to do her homework and a place to store her books, papers, and supplies. Discuss this at a family meeting. Figure out together where your teen will do her work and what cooperation she will need from others to minimize distractions when she is working.

Motion is more distracting than noise, so it is best to be away from TV and from places where there's a lot of coming and going, like the refrigerator. Though complete quiet or background music is probably best for studying, most teens prefer louder music, even while studying. So quiet is not crucial. But since it is difficult to ignore a conversation in the same room, try to choose a place where other conversations are limited.

Rock Music

Often teens listen to rock music while studying and parents feel an almost irresistible urge to make them study in quiet. You may even be aware that some research suggests classical music can promote learning. Despite all this, I think parents should leave this alone. If you feel strongly about it, tell your teen your opinion, and give her your suggestions. But by ninth grade, for most teens, it is too controlling for you to choose when and what music your teen listens to. If you can help your teen surmount the barriers identified earlier, she can and will handle background music responsibly.

Furniture

Your teen should have a large table or desk with enough room to spread out books and papers while working. The furniture stores sell "student desks," so-called because of their small size. Those are too small. A surface at least thirty by sixty inches—the size of an ordinary office desk—is much better. Very sturdy folding tables in that size or larger are available for about $35.

Your teen will also need file folders for each course. If she doesn't have a file drawer, she should get a portable filing box or crate. There are inexpensive plastic filing boxes and crates that are big enough for all her files and supplies, and easy to carry to anyplace in the house where she will be working.

Using Textbooks

Underlining, highlighting, and making notes in the margin of a textbook are useful to the student. But to keep the texts clean so they may be reused, schools forbid students from writing in their texts. Because of that, you should consider buying textbooks for your teen. Helping your teen get the maximum benefit from a year in school—which incidentally costs the state over $4,000— may be well worth spending $100 to $200 for textbooks.

Once you decide to pay for a particular textbook, you might think it would be easiest to let your teen write in the text provided by the school and then pay for the "damage" at the end of the semester. But the school and her teachers may resent your teen's marking of a book in this way. In addition, the school may charge more for a lost or destroyed book than it would cost in a store. So check with the school before approving your teen highlighting, underlining, and writing in a textbook.

Sometimes schools do not have enough books, so students must leave the books in the classroom. If your teen doesn't have her own book or books to take home to study for each course, then you should definitely buy books for her.

If you are buying a book for your teen, get exactly the same edition as is being used in class, so the page numbers and question numbers will match her assignments. If there is no text for a class, try to get a recommendation of a text from the teacher. Even if the teacher says no text is available or needed, your teen will probably benefit from having a textbook on the subject as a reference.

Supplies

Following is a list of the supplies students need. Except for the table and chair, the items don't cost much. Shop for these items with your teen. Pay particular attention to helping your teen get a date book or assignment book that she likes. That may take some shopping around, just as you might do in selecting a date book for yourself. Your teen may want to see what other students are using. Some schools are now providing date books for their students.

From time to time, talk with your teen about any supplies or books that might be helpful. There is a tendency for parents and students to think of buying extra books or supplies as getting an unfair advantage over other students. In a sense it may be unfair, for example, to those who can't afford such extras. Still, it makes sense for you to provide her with every advantage you can. Take time with her to consider buying books, audiotapes, videotapes, and other supplies for learners. Especially in learning a foreign language, additional audiotapes can be a big help.

List of Student Supplies

Table or desk, at least thirty by sixty inches
Chair
Shelf or bookcase
Lamp
Wastebasket
Filing bin, basket, or drawer
File folders
Three-by-five-inch index cards; get five hundred for
   notes, flash cards
File box for the index cards
Watch
Alarm clock
Calculator
Assignment book or date book
Dictionary—*American Heritage, Random House*,
   or *Merriam-Webster*, paperback or hardbound
Thesaurus—paperback or hardbound
Writing-style guide—either *Write Right* by Jan Van-
   olia, or *Elements of Style* by Strunk and White
Knapsack, book bag, or briefcase
Loose-leaf binder
Dividers
Notebook paper
Three-hole punch
Pens
Highlighters
Pencils, pencil sharpener

Eraser
Ruler
Scissors
Transparent tape
Stapler and staples
Paper clips

Typing and Word Processing

Once only secretaries, writers, and some students learned to type. But today, no matter what line of work your teen ultimately goes into, he or she will almost certainly use a computer keyboard. So learning to type is worthwhile for everyone. In school, being able to type will make essay writing quicker and easier. Typed papers may be required in some courses and will be appreciated by teachers in any case.

A word processor or computer costs less than a set of encyclopedias and offers these advantages to any student:

- The typing tutor programs available for computers make learning to type quick and easy.
- Revising and polishing final drafts is much quicker and easier with a word processor.
- Knowing how to use a computer helps in some courses and in using computerized data bases in college libraries.

- Spelling and grammar-checking programs, and an on-line dictionary and thesaurus will help your teen produce better papers and will help rather than impede her writing, spelling, and vocabulary.

Chapter 8 Key Points

1. Get family agreement about where your teen will do her homework. She should be where she will not be distracted by TV or by the movements and conversations of others in the family. She will need a place to spread out her work, and also a place to store her books and papers.
2. Define rules others must follow to minimize distractions.
3. Take your teen shopping for the equipment and supplies she will need.
4. If the school doesn't have texts for every student, buy your teen the textbooks. Even if the school provides books, consider buying them, so she will be able to underline, highlight, and make notes in the margins.
5. A word processor or computer is a valuable tool for a student. Learning to use a computer and to type are useful skills for students and everybody else in today's world.

Chapter 9

Helping Your Teen Deal with the School

So far we've focused almost exclusively on what goes on at home between you and your teen about school and homework. But there are situations in which your role can and should involve action at school. Given the way schools operate and some teens' inability or reluctance to talk to teachers and advisors, you may need to call or visit the school yourself. This chapter provides some suggestions on when and how to do that.

I Hate School

Teens often express negative feelings about school. As regrettable as that is, such comments are often reasonable. Trying to argue your teen out of those feelings won't work. So try to empathize, to accept without necessarily agreeing. Of course, if you actually do agree with a complaint about the school, it will help rather than hurt to say so to your teen.

In addition to specific complaints about particular teachers, assignments, or grades, it is natural to expect teens to have general complaints about school. For one thing, school is work; school is a teen's full-time job. Even the most satisfied and positive adults will sometimes make negative comments about their work. We can't expect our teens not to. And it isn't necessary for parents to react to each of those comments with advice or a lecture about the advantages of education and of a positive attitude.

Also, teens are in the process of becoming independent. So most teens are very sensitive about being controlled or even advised by parents and teachers. And many students feel school is an adversary rather than an institution intended to serve them. They feel frustrated and embarrassed in school. Finally, there is the simple matter of preferring play to schoolwork. So when your teen expresses negative feelings about school, please listen.

Getting Personal Attention

In many high schools, students will get individual attention only if they or their parents make an effort to seek it. This is not due to indifference of the faculty, but just to their work load. High-school teachers generally teach five classes of 20 to 30 students. So a teacher has 100 to 150 or more students for the semester, and literally has only a few minutes per week to focus on each student.

Those few minutes must cover grading the student's assignments and tests, and meetings with the student. Teachers wish this was different.

Counselors and advisers are usually also faced with too many students to spend more than a few hours per year on each student. At this time in California, the typical high-school counselor advises three hundred to five hundred students.

On top of those factors, most teens are reluctant to approach teachers for a private conversation. So when a situation arises in which it seems clear to you that your teen should talk to the teacher, he may resist. Again, this is a situation in which your teen may or may not be high enough up his own learning curve to effectively handle it on his own. If he is, that's terrific. But if he can't, there are many situations in which it is entirely appropriate for you to step in and talk to the teachers yourself.

For example, with his parent's knowledge and consent, Scott was absent from school and missed a test. When he mentioned the test to his science teacher, Mrs. Thorn, she apparently forgot Scott's absence had been arranged in advance. She simply told him, "Well, you know my rule about no makeup exams." Scott's dad was clear that Scott simply had to present his case more clearly and forcibly to Mrs. Thorn. And though Scott kept agreeing that he would talk to her, several weeks passed and he still hadn't done it. He made a variety of excuses about not having time, forgetting, and arguing that it was useless because Mrs. Thorn never gave anyone a break.

Based on the facts, Scott's father could have concluded

that Scott was uninterested in school, forgetful and unorganized, intimidated by Mrs. Thorn, lazy, or just plain stubborn. So he was faced with one of those tough parental decisions. If he left the matter in Scott's hands, Scott might not be able to confront Mrs. Thorn and his science grade might be affected in a significant way. So maybe Scott's dad needed to call or visit Mrs. Thorn. On the other hand, he wanted Scott to learn to speak up for himself and take responsibility. So perhaps he needed to hold back and let Scott face the consequences. He even considered that he might "motivate" Scott to handle the situation by withholding his allowance until Scott talked to Mrs. Thorn.

What Scott's father did was begin by trying to find out what the real problem was. He empathized with Scott: "Scott, it seems you aren't too anxious to talk to Mrs. Thorn about that test." Scott appreciated the tone and absence of advice or questioning, but he was cautious: "Well, she never changes her mind and never bends her rules."

DAD: So you don't think it will do any good.

SCOTT: Yeah. She's really tough. I mean, she's so rigid. She really knows the subject and she can explain it. And I understand all the material. That's why it's so annoying that I'm going to get a C instead of B just because of that missed test.

DAD: That must be real frustrating. You're doing so well in science and then you are penalized because she forgot your absence was excused.

SCOTT: Gosh, I wish I could make her see that, but she won't listen to me.

DAD: She sounds like a pretty tough case.

SCOTT: Well, she is, but she's smart, too. So she always understands what you're trying to say. Maybe if I made an appointment with her and had a copy of the note you originally sent to all my teachers, I could convince her.

In this case, Scott was close enough to competence that just a little moral support got him up for the task. In other cases, Scott may have said, "I know what to say, but there's no way I could do it." In response, his dad might have said, "I understand how you feel. I'd be happy to call her to remind her about the excuse and ask her to let you make up the exam." Even with that offer, Scott might decide to do it himself.

Ultimately, you want your teen to learn to do everything for himself. But that doesn't mean he can do it all now. Just as you did when you first let go of the bicycle seat, you have to decide when to help and when to let go. You'll be best able to make the right choice if you know how your teen feels, and if you use this criterion: *Provide as much help as needed for a high probability of success.*

He's Doing Fine. He's Getting C's

Few people believe most students can master their courses. Administrators, teachers, parents, and students expect grades to have a normal distribution. An exceptionally effective teacher might get a high percentage of his students to master the course. But if he gives out a lot of A's and B's, he will be suspected of being too easy or of "teaching to the test." ("Teaching to the test" taken literally seems sensible enough. Teach students what they need to know and then test that they know it. But in school talk, "teaching to the test" means coaching the students on the test questions, rather than actually teaching them the course. In that sense, teaching to the test is cheating.)

So schools expect lots of students to get C's. If your teen is getting C's, you may get a note that says your teen's test scores indicate he could do better. And particular teachers may comment that your teen could do better with more work and participation. But ordinarily, schools consider C work just fine. They send notices about D's and F's, but not about C's.

To assist your teen in working up to his full potential, you may have to jog the system. Things you might consider going to the school about are:

- Selection of courses
- Selection of teachers
- Arranging your teen's class schedule

- Handling special permissions, such as a missed test
- Dealing with trouble incidents

These will be discussed more fully later, but first let's consider the general issue of parents making demands on the schools.

Many parents sympathize with the teachers. After all, teachers are well-meaning professionals, doing the best they can in trying circumstances and for low pay. Consequently, many parents are reluctant to burden teachers with special requests. In addition, many of us adults tend to revert to a childlike role relative to teachers. If these feelings come up for you, realize that they are very natural and very understandable.

Still, recognize that a school is a large organization, serving many clients. Chances are you will get better treatment by asking for it. Present yourself as a concerned parent, involved in your teen's education. That makes you and the teacher allies. Never use a hostile approach. You may need to be persistent, or even assertive, but you can definitely get things done that would not happen without your intervention.

If your teen winds up with the wrong course or wrong teacher—for him at the present time—get him reassigned. The school may resist such requests, raising objections such as filled classes, setting a precedent for others, or depriving your teen of an important lesson in perseverance. Don't hesitate. The risks are too great that your teen will actually be at a disadvantage in the course and/or be seriously upset about the issue.

If your teen gets into big trouble or even minor scrapes in school, definitely get involved. Trouble can range from a teacher who considers your teen disruptive in class to cutting school to stealing exams. Find out what has happened and what conclusions and actions the school and the teacher have taken. If you agree with the school and teacher, let them know that. Also let them know if you disagree, or if you will investigate and get back to them. After discussing the issue with your teen, figure out what you can do that will most benefit your teen. You might decide to restrict your teen in some way. But more likely your teen will need your support in learning from any mistakes and in limiting the future impact of a negative reputation at school.

Course Selection

I've noted earlier that starting a course without the prerequisites is such a major handicap that it should never be done without very careful consideration. But for a variety of reasons, schools pass many students who are not ready for the next course or grade. One major reason is that teachers know that flunking is discouraging and damaging; it may do more harm than good.

So don't assume the school has carefully considered what is best for your teen. Again, it's not that they don't care. It is simply that they haven't the time to consider every individual in depth. Based on their general philosophy and experience, most schools and teachers apply a particular approach as the one most likely to produce the best results for most students.

But issues like these are highly personal. The impact of repeating a course depends on the individual student and on his understanding of what repeating the course means for and about him. In turn, the teen's feelings will be strongly dependent on what teachers and parents say to him.

Your teen should definitely drop any course for which he does not currently have mastery of the prerequisites. That might mean, for example, that at the start of the present course he should be able to get a B on the final exam of any prerequisite course. This high level of readiness can be relaxed somewhat if the present course will include a review of prerequisite material. But check that the review will be thorough enough and slow enough for your teen.

Other reasons for changing classes are less clear-cut. For example, your teen may tell you he doesn't like a teacher, or the teacher doesn't like him, or none of the students like that teacher. If so, think seriously about getting him changed into another class or, if necessary, letting him drop the class for this semester. Listen carefully to what your teen has to say, and investigate on your own. Meet the teacher, talk to an adviser or counselor about that teacher, and talk to parents whose teens were in that teacher's classes in the past. Based on all the information you gather, decide what you think your teen should do. Then talk to your teen until you both agree on what the best solution would be.

If you and your teen agree that his classes should be changed, then that's your assignment. Most high schools will not readily approve a student's request to change classes. So in most cases you will have to get involved. When you show up with your request, the school faculty and administrators may not be delighted. On the other hand, they are concerned about children and will usually go along with a request from a determined parent. Don't lose time. Don't wait to see how it works out. Call and write; show up in person. Be clear about what you want to happen and that you want it done today or tomorrow.

So if it appears that your teen is being placed in the wrong course, get actively involved. Find out what is happening and why. Talk to your teen. Then make your own decision about the best course selections for your teen. By the junior year, and possibly earlier, you will have to make such decisions jointly with your teen.

Are Some Teachers Better than Others?

Some teachers are definitely more effective than others —their students gain greater knowledge and capability in the subject, like the subject more at the end of the course than they did at the beginning, and feel more confident about learning in that subject or field. Some teachers are more successful for particular types of students. Some teachers do better with top achievers and others with students who need extra help. Find out about your teen's teachers and get your teen together with those that are best for him. Seek those who are well liked and respected by students, parents, and other teachers. Your teen has probably described some teachers as "hard, but good." Obviously you'll want your teen to continue with such teachers. Avoid teachers the students hate. Teachers who give lower grades than the average are either too demanding or their students are learning less. Either way, avoid them.

Learning Styles

Some teachers and educational psychologists today are emphasizing the notion that people have different learning styles. In addition, many learners get some comfort by classifying themselves according to their preferred ways of studying. For example, for learning spelling, presumably some students will do better looking at and visualizing the correct spelling, while others will do better with phonics and hearing the spelling.

However, as we've emphasized all along, the only way to learn anything is by practice. In most cases, the task demands a specific type of practice. Visual, auditory, and tactile learners all must solve algebra problems to learn algebra; they must write essays in order to master that ability. And, once again, almost everyone can master all the courses in high school. Don't dwell on your teen's learning style. Just guide him to do the practice appropriate to each subject.

Chapter 9 Key Points

1. The school is not equipped to look after every student's individual best interests. You may have to help your teen handle some administrative issues.

2. Your teen may resist your getting involved. You shouldn't necessarily stay away for that reason.

3. Be sure your teen has the prerequisites for each of his courses.

4. Discuss your teen's course load with him and with other parents, students, teachers, and counselors. Arrive at your own judgment about what is best, reach an agreement with your teen, then do what you have to in order to get the school to go along.

5. Not all teachers are equally effective for your teen. If there seems to be a problem, take action promptly.

6. Do not make your teen stay with the wrong course or the wrong teacher to learn perseverance. School has many elements of being a contest. Even with every possible bit of assistance from you, succeeding in school is sufficiently challenging for him to develop perseverance.

7. If your teen is actually hopelessly behind in a course, let him drop it. You may have to help get the school to approve that move.

Appendix

Watch for Progress

In Chapter 3, I suggested that you complete a questionnaire about your teen's current performance in school and at home. Another copy of that questionnaire is provided beginning on the next page. Many parents have found it useful to fill out the questionnaire again from time to time. By showing that you and your teen are moving in the right direction and by highlighting his and your successes, noting his progress will provide motivation to continue doing what works and changing what doesn't.

If you like the idea of using the questionnaire, you may want to make several photocopies so you will have blanks for future use.

Questionnaire

For each item, check the frequency with which your teen
does this. Then check your rating of his performance of
this item.

	Frequency				Rating		
	Never	Seldom	Usually	Always	Out-standing	Satis-factory	Needs improvement
In School							
Attends classes	☐	☐	☐	☐	☐	☐	☐
Knows what is required	☐	☐	☐	☐	☐	☐	☐
Participates in class	☐	☐	☐	☐	☐	☐	☐
Gets along with teachers	☐	☐	☐	☐	☐	☐	☐
Asks for help when needed	☐	☐	☐	☐	☐	☐	☐
Learns subjects thoroughly	☐	☐	☐	☐	☐	☐	☐
Enjoys school	☐	☐	☐	☐	☐	☐	☐
Participates in school activities	☐	☐	☐	☐	☐	☐	☐
Feels able to succeed	☐	☐	☐	☐	☐	☐	☐
In Doing Homework							
Knows the assignments	☐	☐	☐	☐	☐	☐	☐
Gets started promptly	☐	☐	☐	☐	☐	☐	☐
Works steadily	☐	☐	☐	☐	☐	☐	☐
Does it well	☐	☐	☐	☐	☐	☐	☐
Turns it in on time	☐	☐	☐	☐	☐	☐	☐
Asks for help when needed	☐	☐	☐	☐	☐	☐	☐
Knows how to study for each subject	☐	☐	☐	☐	☐	☐	☐

	Frequency				Rating		
	Never	Seldom	Usually	Always	Out-standing	Satis-factory	Needs improvement
Plans ahead for large assignments	☐	☐	☐	☐	☐	☐	☐
Manages time well	☐	☐	☐	☐	☐	☐	☐
Is well organized	☐	☐	☐	☐	☐	☐	☐
At Home							
Gets along with family	☐	☐	☐	☐	☐	☐	☐
Talks things over with parents	☐	☐	☐	☐	☐	☐	☐
Tells the truth	☐	☐	☐	☐	☐	☐	☐
Enjoys friends	☐	☐	☐	☐	☐	☐	☐
Enjoys recreational activities	☐	☐	☐	☐	☐	☐	☐
Sets goals	☐	☐	☐	☐	☐	☐	☐
Achieves his goals	☐	☐	☐	☐	☐	☐	☐
Does his chores	☐	☐	☐	☐	☐	☐	☐
Behaves responsibly	☐	☐	☐	☐	☐	☐	☐
Has a job	☐	☐	☐	☐	☐	☐	☐
Feels successful	☐	☐	☐	☐	☐	☐	☐

Do You Need to Have Your Teen Tested for Learning Disabilities?

This book is for parents of students who should be succeeding in regular high-school classes. If you have any reason to suspect your teen is mentally, physically, or emotionally unable to succeed in regular classes, you and your teen may need special assistance to evaluate him, and possibly might need to provide tutoring or treatment. Such evaluations are best left to the experts.

Following are a few signals that may help you decide whether or not to have your teen evaluated for learning disabilities.

These things tend to rule out learning disabilities and, in fact, usually indicate the ability to succeed in regular classes:

- Does well in some major subjects.
- Did well in school up to the seventh or eighth grade or beyond.
- Does well with some teachers.
- Easily learns and remembers words to songs or sports statistics.
- Clever in learning a hobby or board games.
- Reads and understands books or magazines on a favorite topic.
- Concentrates on things of interest, such as a movie, a video game, or a hobby.

These are things that suggest the possibility of a learning disability:

- Has a vision or hearing problem.
- Is unable to read the newspaper or understand what he's read.
- Prefers to have someone read the textbook to him, rather than reading it himself.
- Has unusual difficulty with spelling.
- Frequently mixes up phone numbers.
- Has had difficulties in school from the first or second grade.
- Can't remember multiplication tables.

- Can't memorize or remember the words to songs or poems.
- Can't sit still and concentrate on things of interest, such as a movie, a video game, or a hobby.

If you decide to consult a learning disabilities professional, a good place to start is at your teen's high school. Most large high schools or districts have learning specialists and counselors who can either do testing and evaluations themselves or refer you to outside experts. Two other good sources of recommendations are your family doctor and the Learning Disabilities Association in your city or county.

Other Problems

Many teens and their families are dealing with stresses that interfere with school performance—things like:

- Separation or divorce of parents
- Sickness or death of a family member or friend
- Drug or alcohol abuse
- Child abuse or molestation

If any of these things are going on in your teen's life, start dealing with them; this is a higher priority than improving his study habits or grades.

Reading Skills

Reading is the primary learning skill for schoolwork. So it pays to be certain that your teen can read quickly enough and with adequate comprehension to handle his high-school work. Don't guess about this. In the noteworthy *Serano v. Priest* lawsuit, a straight-C high-school graduate sued the school district in Compton, California. He claimed his constitutional rights had been infringed because he had gotten passing grades all through school but had not learned to read. (He was not dyslexic.) He won the case.

Unless your teen has a learning disability, he can and should learn to read at or above his grade level and at three hundred to four hundred words per minute by the twelfth grade. If you don't know whether he is reading at his grade level, start by getting his test scores from the school. If for some reason his test results are unavailable or seem questionable, use the reading comprehension test that follows.

This test, the Ohio Literacy Test of Reading Comprehension, takes just five minutes and it is quite accurate in checking reading comprehension. It was developed for the state of Ohio more than fifty years ago and has, over the years, been compared to many newer, more extensive tests. The test has been shown to be completely satisfactory for determining whether high-school students have adequate reading comprehension. The test is easy for you to score. The scoring key for the test immediately follows it.

If your teen's reading comprehension is not at his grade level and he doesn't have a learning disability, a small amount of remedial tutoring should quickly bring him up to his grade level. As a rough estimate, he can probably bring his reading comprehension level up one year for every twenty hours of work.

You might also test how fast he can read. Time him as he reads from a novel for exactly three minutes. Then count the number of words he read and divide by three. In counting the words, you can save time by counting the lines and multiplying by the number of words in a typical line.

If he is not reading at least two hundred words per minute when entering high school and at least three hundred words per minute when he enters college, he should take a speed-reading course or use a self-help book on speed-reading. Students can generally increase their reading speed to four hundred words per minute or more in just a few hours of training. In addition to increased speed, such training also increases comprehension.

Reading-improvement courses for high-school students are often available through high schools and community colleges. In addition, there are private individuals and companies that provide tutoring or classes for small groups. There are also excellent self-help books to guide a student in doing the practice necessary to improve his reading speed and comprehension. Though this takes more self-discipline, it is very economical and can be quite effective.

Ohio Literacy Test of Reading Comprehension

This is a five-minute test to see how well you can understand what you read. The questions start easy and get harder as you go along. You are not expected to be able to answer all of them, but do as many as you can. Do not guess. If you do not know the right answer to a question, skip it. There are no "catch" questions.

Read each question carefully. If the right answer is "Yes," draw a ring around "Yes." If the answer is "No," draw a ring around "No."

There are fifty questions. Complete as many as you can in exactly five minutes.

For example: Do cats bark?   No   Yes

The answer, of course, is "No," so you should draw a circle around "No."

1. Can you see? .... No   Yes
2. Do men eat stone? .... No   Yes
3. Do boys like to play? .... No   Yes
4. Can a bed run? .... No   Yes
5. Have books hands? .... No   Yes
6. Is ice hot? .... No   Yes
7. Do winds blow? .... No   Yes

8. Have all girls the same name? .... No   Yes
9. Is warm clothing good for winter? .... No   Yes
10. Is this page of paper white? .... No   Yes
11. Is every young woman a teacher? .... No   Yes
12. Is it always perfect weather? .... No   Yes
13. Is the heart within the body? .... No   Yes
14. Are railroad tickets free? .... No   Yes
15. Are summer days ordinarily cold? .... No   Yes
16. Do clerks enjoy a vacation? .... No   Yes
17. Is the President a public official? .... No   Yes
18. Would you enjoy the loss of a fortune? .... No   Yes
19. Does an auto sometimes need repair? ...... No   Yes
20. Is it important to remember
    commands? .... No   Yes
21. Are avenues usually paved with
    oxygen? .... No   Yes
22. Do we desire serious trouble? .... No   Yes
23. Are muzzles usually noticeable? .... No   Yes
24. Is practical judgment valuable? .... No   Yes
25. Ought a man's career to be ruined by
    accidents? .... No   Yes
26. Do you cordially recommend forgery? ..... No   Yes
27. Does an emergency require immediate
    decision? .... No   Yes
28. Are gradual improvements worth-
    while? .... No   Yes
29. Should honesty involve personal
    misfortune? .... No   Yes
30. Is a punctual person continually tardy? .... No   Yes
31. Are all human beings mortal? .... No   Yes

32. Does a sportive person necessarily have "nerve"? .... No   Yes
33. Are instantaneous effects invariably rapid? .... No   Yes
34. Should preliminary disappointment discourage you? .... No   Yes
35. Is hearsay testimony trustworthy evidence? .... No   Yes
36. Are the best authorities characterized by wisdom? .... No   Yes
37. Is extreme athletic exercise surely necessary? .... No   Yes
38. Is incessant discussion usually boresome? .... No   Yes
39. Are algebraic symbols ever found in formulae? .... No   Yes
40. Are tentative regulations often estimable? .... No   Yes
41. Are "diminutive" and "Lilliputian" absolutely identical? .... No   Yes
42. Is an infinitesimal titanic bulk possible? ... No   Yes
43. Do all connubial unions eventuate felicitously? .... No   Yes
44. Is a gelatinous exultation ridiculous? .... No   Yes
45. Are "perambulate" and "meander" similar in meaning? .... No   Yes
46. Is avarice sometimes exhibited by cameos? .... No   Yes
47. Are steep ascents usually coexistent with sharp declivities? .... No   Yes

48. Are the laity apt to indulge in radical
    theosophies? .... No   Yes
49. Is it necessary to know dialect forms
    in order to speak patois? .... No   Yes
50. Does a carnivorous quadruped devour
    fronds indiscriminately? .... No   Yes

Scoring Key

The correct answers appear below. Mark questions right
or wrong. Skipped questions are marked wrong. Continue until you encounter three wrong (or skipped) answers in a row. Note the number of the last question the
student got right, and interpret his score from the table
below.

1. YES	14. NO	27. YES	39. YES
2. NO	15. NO	28. YES	40. YES
3. YES	16. YES	29. NO	41. NO
4. NO	17. YES	30. NO	42. NO
5. NO	18. NO	31. YES	43. NO
6. NO	19. YES	32. NO	44. YES
7. YES	20. YES	33. YES	45. YES
8. NO	21. NO	34. NO	46. NO
9. YES	22. NO	35. NO	47. YES
10. YES	23. YES	36. YES	48. NO
11. NO	24. YES	37. NO	49. NO
12. NO	25. NO	38. YES	50. NO
13. YES	26. NO		

Last Correct Before 3 Misses	Grade Level
3–4	1
5–10	2
11–15	3
16–19	4
20–22	5
23–24	6
25–27	7
28–29	8
30–32	9
33	10
34	11
35–36	12
37 or more	Above 12

Notes on Note-taking

There are many opinions about the value of lecture notes and how to take them. As a result, we've seen many students who are either following or resisting well-meaning but misleading advice. So here are some facts about note-taking you may want to consider.

Extensive research on note-taking at the University of Minnesota showed that the best students took brief notes, focusing on trying to get the main ideas from lectures.

In contrast, the weakest students tried to write down as much as they could of the lecture, hoping to be able to learn the material later.

Tape-recording a lecture is overdoing the wrong idea. If a student misses a lecture or has a reading problem, a tape can help. But as a way to review the material in a lecture, listening to a tape is inefficient compared to reviewing brief notes on the main points.

Based on the research, the best advice on note-taking is this:

- Divide a piece of paper into two columns, labeled "Key Ideas" and "Main Facts." Listen to the lecture. When you hear something that falls in either of those two categories, write a brief note in the appropriate column.
- As soon as possible after the lecture, use your notes and your memory to reconstruct the main ideas presented. If necessary, add to or modify your notes.
- Also review the key facts while the lecture is fresh in your mind. If necessary, add to or revise your notes.

Special Note on Algebra

Algebra is the single most troublesome course for high-school students. Difficulties with algebra convince most students to stay away from careers in such areas as accounting, economics, engineering, and science. Many students become convinced that they are not smart and should avoid all intellectual pursuits, including college.

Even if you don't remember or have never learned algebra, here are a few tips that may help you help your teen with it:

- Algebra is sophisticated and abstract. Just as younger children need a certain level of maturity before they are ready to read, it seems there is a similar threshold of mental maturity for algebra. The pre-algebra courses offered for high-school freshmen provide teens who need it an extra year to mature. If your teen has not excelled in math, don't insist that your teen take algebra in the eighth or ninth grade.
- Algebra is difficult to teach because people who can attack problems correctly often have difficulty describing to others what gives them that insight. This poses great difficulties in tutoring. The tutor tries to explain. The student frequently finds the explanation confusing and seemingly different than the explanation offered in class. This frequently upsets both the tutor and the student. If you know algebra, keep this in mind if your teen asks you for help.
- Algebra involves the cumulative learning of methods and techniques. Once a student gets behind even a little, it is almost impossible to catch up. Algebra teachers know this and try to assist stu-

dents by being strict about daily homework. But in algebra more than in any other subject, mastering the assignments is essential. Many students who were successful in earlier math courses and have been doing their homework are surprised when they get into difficulty with algebra. Many of them then jump to the false conclusion that they are no good at math.

■ Knowledge of fractions is an absolute prerequisite for algebra. Unfortunately, most students passed math throughout middle school without mastering fractions. This hinders them in learning to manipulate algebraic notation, so they get lost and fall behind. Compounding the problem is that the student thinks the difficulty is entirely based on the new material and therefore never realizes that he needs to learn or review fractions. *Before he starts algebra, be sure your teen can add, subtract, multiply, divide, and simplify fractions.*

Bibliography

Bloom, Benjamin S. *All Our Children Learning: A Primer for Parents, Teachers, and Other Educators*. New York: McGraw-Hill (1982).

Bowsher, Jack E. *Educating America—Lessons Learned in the Nation's Corporations*. New York: Wiley (1989).

Dinkmeyer, Don, and Gary D. McKay. *Systematic Training for Effective Parenting—Teen*. Circle Pines, MN: American Guidance Service (1983).

Ginot, Haim G. *Between Parent and Teen*. New York: Avon Books (1969).

Gordon, Thomas. *Parent Effectiveness Training*. San Diego: McKay (1970).

Gould, Steven J. *The Mismeasure of Man*. New York: Norton (1983).

Sizer, Theodore R. *Horace's School: Redesigning the American High School*. New York: Houghton Mifflin (1992).

Turecki, Stanley. *The Difficult Child*. New York: Bantam Books (1989).

———. "Temperamentally Difficult Children." *Feelings, 32 (1)*: Ross Laboratories (1990).